RANTS AND REVELATIONS FROM A NOT-SO-PROPER SOUTHERN LADY

SUSANNAH B. LEWIS

NELSON
BOOKS

An Imprint of Thomas Nelson

Published in Nashville, Tennessee, by Nelson Books, an imprint of Thomas Nelson. Nelson Books and Thomas Nelson are registered trademarks of HarperCollins Christian Publishing, Inc.

Published in association with Jessica Kirkland and the literary agency of Kirkland Media Management, LLC, P.O. Box 1539, Liberty, TX 77575.

Thomas Nelson titles may be purchased in bulk for educational, business, fund-raising, or sales promotional use. For information, please e-mail SpecialMarkets@ThomasNelson.com.

Unless otherwise noted, Scripture quotations are taken from the Holy Bible, New International Version®, NIV®. Copyright © 1973, 1978, 1984, 2011 by Biblica, Inc.® Used by permission of Zondervan. All rights reserved worldwide. www.Zondervan.com. The "NIV" and "New International Version" are trademarks registered in the United States Patent and Trademark Office by Biblica, Inc.®

Scripture quotations marked THE MESSAGE are from *The Message*. Copyright © by Eugene H. Peterson 1993, 1994, 1995, 1996, 2000, 2001, 2002. Used by permission of NavPress. All rights reserved. Represented by Tyndale House Publishers, Inc.

Scripture quotations marked NASB are from New American Standard Bible®. Copyright © 1960, 1962, 1963, 1968, 1971, 1972, 1973, 1975, 1977, 1995 by The Lockman Foundation. Used by permission. (www.Lockman.org)

Scripture quotations marked NKJV are from the New King James Version®. © 1982 by Thomas Nelson. Used by permission. All rights reserved.

Scripture quotations marked TLB are from The Living Bible. Copyright © 1971. Used by permission of Tyndale House Publishers, Inc., Carol Stream, Illinois 60188. All rights reserved.

Scripture quotations marked ESV are from the ESV® Bible (The Holy Bible, English Standard Version®), copyright © 2001 by Crossway, a publishing ministry of Good News Publishers. Used by permission. All rights reserved.

Any Internet addresses, phone numbers, or company or product information printed in this book are offered as a resource and are not intended in any way to be or to imply an endorsement by Thomas Nelson, nor does Thomas Nelson vouch for the existence, content, or services of these sites, phone numbers, companies, or products beyond the life of this book.

ISBN 978-1-4002-0805-0 (eBook)
ISBN 978-1-4002-0804-3 (TP)

Library of Congress Cataloging-in-Publication Data

Names: Lewis, Susannah B., 1981- author.
Title: How may I offend you today? : rants and revelations from a
    not-so-proper southern lady / Susannah B. Lewis.
Description: Nashville, Tennessee : Nelson Books, 2020. | Summary: "Lewis
    turns her trademark humor to ordinary events that work her nerves--from
    people who wear t-shirts with indecent images to public displays of
    affection in the plumbing aisle of Lowe's--while keeping a wry eye on
    herself and her own temptation to vent grievances "like a teenage girl
    in overalls and Birkenstocks.""-- Provided by publisher.
Identifiers: LCCN 2020009896 | ISBN 9781400208043 (trade paperback) | ISBN
    9781400208050 (ebook)
Subjects: LCSH: Lewis, Susannah B., 1981- | Christian biography--United
    States. | Christian life--Humor. | Christian life--Anecdotes.
Classification: LCC BR1725.L4355 A3 2020 | DDC 277.3/083092 [B]--dc23
LC record available at https://lccn.loc.gov/2020009896

Printed in the United States of America

20 21 22 23 24 LSC 10 9 8 7 6 5 4 3 2 1

Contents

"I'm a nobody that's tryin' to tell everybody 'bout Somebody that can save anybody."

—DENVER MOORE, *SAME KIND OF DIFFERENT AS ME*

"Susannah Lewis is a breath of fresh air. Her writing is insightful, hilarious, and full of all the things we think but are often afraid to say out loud. You will close the pages of this book and feel like you've made a new best friend."

—MELANIE SHANKLE, *NEW YORK TIMES* BESTSELLING AUTHOR OF *ON THE BRIGHT SIDE*

"My friend Susannah's new book is a refreshing and honest look at motherhood, marriage, and sisterhood. And to top it off, she speaks in the voice of a Southern lady who deeply loves Jesus. I can totally relate to that!"

—MISS KAY ROBERTSON, MATRIARCH OF THE ROBERTSON FAMILY, AUTHOR OF *MISS KAY'S DUCK COMMANDER KITCHEN*, AND STAR OF *DUCK DYNASTY*

"Whenever my mama was tickled by someone's outspokenness, she would grin—maybe even clap her hands—and say, 'Oh, she is a pistol.' It was one of Mama's favorite terms of endearment. And so here is what I want to tell you now that I've read *How May I Offend You Today?*: I have never been more convinced that Susannah Lewis is, in fact, a pistol. She is outspoken, she is hilarious, and she is really not at all concerned with whether any of us happen to agree with her views on pajama bottoms or electronics or how to navigate the carpool lane, among other things. But underneath all Susannah's funny fire and sass, there is such tenderness—such deep affection for family and faith and loving people really well. So while you may show up to this book for the hot takes, you'll leave encouraged and reminded of the kindness and care of our very good God. Mama would tell us that's a win all the way around."

—SOPHIE HUDSON, AUTHOR OF *STAND ALL THE WAY UP* AND CO-HOST OF *THE BIG BOO CAST*

"This should be required reading for every human immediately exiting the baptismal, prior to heading to the potluck. Susannah Lewis is a master wordsmith, comedic legend, and the quintessential anti-Pharisee. Were it a different time and place, this is one of the women Jesus would butter biscuits with. She breaks all the rules put in place by the pompous and is the united voice of the masses, who don't have the guts or the drawl to say what needs to be said so that we all might feel normal. *How May I Offend You Today?* is laugh-out-loud funny, with wisdom and raw realness that validated the voices in my head and confirmed my belief in the power of authenticity. No offense comes from the Lord; lucky for us, He anointed Susannah to pen it with humor, wit, and wisdom."

—JAMI AMERINE, AUTHOR OF *STOLEN JESUS*
AND *SACRED GROUND, STICKY FLOORS*

Dear Reader,

I completed this manuscript in February 2019, a few weeks before our baby girl was born. With Cheeto-stained fingers, I spent many late nights on my couch (stifling burps from indigestion and other horrific noises my body made) working to get this book finished before she was placed on my chest covered in goo and preciousness.

February 2019 now seems like eons ago, doesn't it?

As I wrote this book, I'd never heard of coronavirus (sounds like slang for "hangover"). *Tiger King* would've likely been an animated *Lion King* spin-off instead the craziest documentary I would ever see. My children were in a classroom instead of downloading the Zoom app at our dining table. Protests didn't fill every news hour. Law enforcement, for the most part, was revered and respected. The murder hornet was only an idea for a sci-fi movie. Life was very different for all of us when I typed the last words of this book. Therefore, I recognize readers may possess a different mindset now than when the book was completed last year—a mindset featuring all the Devil's favorite emotions: worry, panic, anger, sadness, anxiety, etc.

The purpose in writing *How May I Offend You Today?* was to encourage people to stand up for what they believe in, even when it isn't popular. (Which I believe is more of a needed reminder now than just a few months ago.) Saint Paul said that if he wanted the approval of people, he wouldn't be a servant of Christ. Paul nailed it. If what I say and believe offends someone, yet it aligns with

God's Word, I don't lose much sleep over it. I don't want to offend God, and that's that.

Paul was persecuted for speaking truth. He was locked in a prison cell. He continued to speak. He was beaten. He continued to speak. God fought for him. Paul didn't shut up because some people hated him or disagreed with him or found what he said to be "offensive." And because he spoke, slaves were set free and Jew and Gentile alike came to know Christ.

You have every right (and even a duty) to stand up and speak what you believe in. That right isn't only designated for some. The First Amendment applies to you too. Don't forget that. Don't roll over. Don't be silenced. Stand firm and speak your stance (in love, always in love) when necessary. Welcome healthy debate and open-minded conversation but walk away, nobly, from heated argument.

Know who you are in Christ alone. Don't let anyone give you a name that isn't yours. Not racist. Not judgmental. Not bigot. Not quack. Not hillbilly. Not idiot. Not uneducated. Not close-minded.

Unfortunately, we now live in the age of "cancel culture." People adamantly refuse to have an open mind to what others have to say. They find offense where there is none—or at least where none would have been found a few months ago. Our differences seem to divide instead of unify. Free speech can be inaccurately deemed as hate. So many have a heart problem—not living to please Him. Not living in peace. Not living in love. We are all guilty of offending Him with our words, actions, and beliefs.

Aside from our words and actions, I believe our lack of empathy is also offensive to Him. And so, I'd like to make it clear, that although I stand firm in my beliefs (politically, spiritually, morally) and say things with sass and crass, I do empathize with those who have walked a different road than I have walked.

But you know what the beautiful thing is? We don't have to agree on every single thing. As you read this book, maybe you'll be offended. Maybe you'll think I worded something a little too harshly or without tact. You may shake your head and declare that I am wrong, especially in today's tumultuous times. That's your right.

I will eagerly admit, as a sinner through and through who relies on His grace and forgiveness hourly (minutely), I know I offend God. I repent. I try to do better tomorrow. I know I offend others too. But I strive to always cling to His Word instead of the world and what it expects me to do or say.

The bottom line is, if you've accepted Jesus as your Savior, you're still going to see me in heaven one day. You won't be ducking behind a cloud to avoid me, because what I've written in this book that got you all hot and bothered won't amount to a thing.

The Bible says we won't know the day or hour when our Jesus will return, descending on a cloud to join us all together with Him, but I have to think all the panic and unrest going on in the world today is expediting it little by little. Mercy, I can't wait to get to heaven. There will be no more dissension or anger or malice or hurt. No worry or anxiety or fear. No one will be offended. We will be consumed, instead, with absolute peace and love and acceptance in the presence of our magnificent Savior.

Until that time comes, do all that you can to make heaven a place on earth. (Extra points if you sang that in Belinda Carlisle's voice.)

Love each other. Be good to each other. Point people to Him. Stand on His Word. Stand on His Truth. Strive to please Him alone. You may fail, but accept His grace and keep going.

Love,
Susannah

Introduction

Why Is Nobody Else Losing It?

I'm so thankful Al Gore invented the internet. Now regular ol' ordinary people like me can make a silly video with my phone and upload it to Facebook or YouTube, where it magically travels through some wires and tunnels in an underworld I imagine is like in *The Matrix*, and suddenly a million people know who I am. It's real trippy stuff.

I remember being ten years old, sitting on our floral couch and holding a blue Bic pen. I passionately wrote a twelve-page novel about two friends, Laura and Sarah, while my mother watched the newly released flick *The War of the Roses* on VHS, feeling lucky she'd snagged it from Ticket to the Hits (our local video store) on a Friday night. While Barbara and Oliver hung from a chandelier on our Quasar console television screen, I scribbled my story on wide-ruled notebook paper and dreamt of being a published author.

On the backs of many homemade books, I wrote four-star reviews (not five-star because I was a humble kid) and drew *New York Times* Best Seller stamps. I asked my English teacher how a person became an author, and of course she never once mentioned talking into a Samsung cellular phone and uploading the video to "social media." If she had, I probably would have nervously twitched in my jelly shoes and assumed she was speaking Rangpuri or something. If she had mentioned "going viral," I would have slowly backed away and assumed she needed some soup and a nap.

But that's exactly how it came to be that you're reading these words right now. I sat in front of my phone's camera and rambled about various happenings in my life. Then I took a deep breath and uploaded the clips to the World Wide Web. People actually liked those videos and shared them with friends, and their friends shared them with more friends, and I caught the attention of a literary agent and here we are.

Again, it's real trippy stuff.

How many absolutely hilarious social-media moms are posting online? How many blog posts are published daily by women with stale Tater Tots between the seats of their SUV and Superman Underoos with skid marks in their laundry basket? I am going to guestimate 18.4 quadrillion. So what in the world made me stand out? What made my posts go viral? I have wondered that often.

It might have something to do with my tagline, "Whoa! Susannah." In home economics class way back in 1998, I said something brutally honest. I wish I could remember what I said, but a hush fell over the classroom, and all eyes were off the sewing machines and on me standing there in overalls and Steve Madden wedges. A classmate interrupted the silence by singing, "Whoa! Susannah" to the tune of "Oh, Susannah."

Whoa! I had said out loud what they were all thinking. And that's what I continue to do with my blogs and vlogs. If you google my name, results such as "Social Media Mom Says What We Won't" and "Tennessee Mom's Rant Goes Viral" pop up.

Of course, there are people who disagree with every word that comes from my fingers and mouth, and that's quite all right, but some people find what I say refreshing. They find humorous honesty inspirational, and my random rants and revelations encourage them to speak up about what they believe to be true as well.

They might even agree with me that we live in a hypersensitive, overly politically correct society. They probably notice that I can't say much of anything without someone getting offended. Of course, I don't condone bullying or degrading others, but I believe people are too dad-gum sensitive and uptight these days and need to remove the corncob from whatever orifice it is obstructing.

Recently I was at Walmart around nine thirty in the morning and gawked at the number of people walking around in pajama pants. I'm not talking about *athleisure* (I love that word) garments. I am talking about legit fleece Marvin the Martian pants that drag the floor or flannels that say "Sleep" across the rear. If you're going to wear those, shouldn't you be someplace where sleeping is the goal? Good grief. I know it was early, but is anyone so lethargic and incoherent they can't slip on a pair of real pants? I hadn't seen that many people wearing pajama pants at once since I was at a slumber party in eighth grade.

> I believe people are too dad-gum sensitive and uptight these days and need to remove the corncob from whatever orifice it is obstructing.

After I left the store, I made a video about what I'd seen and then posted it to YouTube. The majority of commenters agreed with me. "Girl, yes! Preach!" However, some people took the rant entirely too personally. I got one e-mail that read, "I don't appreciate your rude and judgmental video about people wearing pajama pants to Walmart." To which I responded, in typical Whoa! Susannah fashion (pun intended), "You wear pajama pants to Walmart, don't you?"

Honestly, I didn't intend to be rude and judgmental. I never do. Sister, you go ahead and wear your private garments in public. Do what you want. I'm not judging you as a person. I just don't prefer a cup of flannel and highly flammable tea in public. But if someone else does, you can bet your britches I'm going to give my opinion about it. It's who I am.

As a Christian, though, I do want to be careful when I share my opinion or my humor. We will one day be held accountable for every word we speak. I will admit I have posted videos or written posts featuring what I thought was a humorous rant, only to be convicted by the Holy Spirit and delete it. It is really easy to start off with good intentions but end up being too harsh and critical about another person, which is never pleasing to God. I often pray, "Lord, don't let my jokes turn anyone away from You or hurt my witness." But I also think humor can bring people closer to God.

God uses satire in the Scriptures. In Jeremiah 46:11–12 He tells the hardheaded Egyptians they can go ahead and waste all their time climbing a mountain for some of their fancy, magical healing balm if they must, even though it's not going to work. And in 1 Kings Elijah taunts the Baal prophets by saying of their false god, "Call a little louder—he is a god, after all. Maybe he's off meditating somewhere or other, or maybe he's gotten involved in a project, or maybe he's on vacation. You don't suppose he's overslept, do you, and needs to be waked up?" (18:27–28 THE MESSAGE). The Bible is, of course, our manual for living and should be taken seriously, but Elijah made me laugh out loud with that roast.

In Proverbs 17:22, our Lord tells us that a joyful heart is good medicine. He delights in laughter and comedy. We are made in His image, after all, and we are most certainly able to identify and convey humor, aren't we? (Most of us, anyway.) However, as I said before, there's a fine line that can easily be crossed. Lord knows I've unintentionally crossed it. Some people show me grace when I cross the line and some people don't.

Some who disagree with my beliefs and opinions let me know with venom and spitfire in the comments section on my blog or on Facebook. I envision the writer as a woman with her forehead vein bulging, a cigarette hanging from her mouth, angrily pounding on her keyboard before she sticks a needle into the leg of a voodoo doll that resembles me. But I'm okay with that. I'm okay with not pleasing all of the people all of the time.

Luckily, God not only gives us senses of humor but also gives us the wisdom and knowledge we need in the Bible to walk that line—if we listen to Him, that is. He calls us to encourage one another with truth and the good news, but He also instructs us to stand firm and never waver from the Scriptures, even if doing so doesn't make us popular. If what we say aligns with the Word of God, we're told to shout it from the rooftops.

So follow me up to the roof, will you?

I have a few jokes to crack, rants to go on, and truths to tell.

**THINGS THAT WORK
MY NERVES #11**

Public displays of affection

I understand how in love you are. I've been there.
But never, under any circumstances, should
you tongue-clean your partner's teeth in
the plumbing aisle of a Lowe's.

Chapter One

Common Sense
Isn't Common

My nine-year-old son, Bennett, and I were sitting in the waiting room at the car dealership one day while my vehicle underwent maintenance. We'd been there for darn near two hours, and our nerves were shot. Bennett was in a hot panic because his beloved iPod was running low on juice (this was before his electronics detox, which I'll talk about later), and I was in a panic because a certain daytime talk show I loathe was on the television in the corner, and I would rather hear Freddy Krueger massage a chalkboard than listen to the host's voice.

I looked up to see a man walk into the service department in a T-shirt that would make Chelsea Handler clutch her pearls. The f-bomb was plastered across his chest in large and bold letters above a sexually graphic illustration. As you've read, I am not easily offended, but I certainly did not want my innocent boy to see such vulgarity. I did not want to hear, "Mama, what are those people *doing* on that man's shirt?" So before Bennett could notice, I summoned him to follow me and we walked out of the service department.

It was a sunshiny day, so we strolled around the car lot and beat off the hungry sharks. I was not interested in a new, fully loaded Tahoe for zero down and low financing. I just wanted to escape the obscenities in the service department waiting room.

While we walked around the lot and the boy begged me to get a new SUV with DVD players built into the headrests, I was reminded of a time a few years back when a man at the community ball field had on a similar shirt. His lovely attire featured the spelled-out equivalent of "Eff You" in bold print above an extended middle finger. He was asked to leave the family-friendly location crowded with children, and he had the nerve to become irate and shout about freedom of expression and freedom of speech. Ironically, he never actually shouted, "Eff you," or threw up his middle finger.

I was furious with these two idiots. Who in the world thinks it is acceptable to wear something so obscene at a youth baseball game or on a Monday morning at an automotive dealership? Save that explicit attire for the club on Saturday night, when inebriated adults will find it humorous.

When I was a teenager, I had a T-shirt with a marijuana plant wearing dreadlocks and a Jamaican beanie on the back of it. I smoked pot once and felt the need to spend my hard-earned babysitting money on that tee when I saw it at a beachside shop in Florida. I was too scared to wear the shirt though. I certainly didn't want my mother or grandmother or the little kids I watched in the nursery at church to see me wearing a shirt with weed on it. Even at seventeen, I had enough common sense to know it was better suited for me to wear to bed in the privacy of my own room.

When I was that same silly teenager, I also listened to explicit lyrics. Even today, when I'm folding laundry, twelve stanzas from a Snoop Dogg tune will pop into my head, and I am surprised that

I miraculously remember every foul word. Although I loved Snoop Dogg and listened to him on repeat, I never ever pulled up to a gas station with it blaring for the little kid in the back of his mother's van parked at the adjacent pump to hear. Again, even at seventeen, I had enough common sense to know better.

As I so often do when I'm perturbed with something, I voiced my opinion about the service department scenario on my blog. The comments section of the post was filled with remarks from intelligent individuals who agreed with my stance that exposing the public to this kind of foul stupidity was ridiculous.

But there were a few—*a few*—who disagreed with my abhorrence of the situation. Like the moron at the ball field several years back, they believed it was perfectly appropriate for a person to wear such a shirt in a public place where children are likely to be present—not to mention the poor elderly lady who just wanted the oil changed in her 1992 Buick Century but was forced instead to witness the vulgar sex act depicted on that stranger's chest. Bless her heart. She had to have been blushing beneath all of her rouge—and possibly having flashbacks of her trip to Woodstock in 1969.

Some of those commenters argued it was extremely judgmental of me to complain about what another person wears. I was "an entitled mother who thinks the world revolves around her precious kids" and I should "grow up." People who wear obscene T-shirts shouldn't have to think about little old me or my innocent children when picking out their wardrobe.

I thought the arguments from those people were so ignorant that I could barely bring myself to respond without using the very expletives I'd seen on that fine young gentleman's shirt. That would have been very hypocritical of me, wouldn't it? And yet I would never use those words in front of a child or a grandmother, and I especially wouldn't broadcast them across my chest on a Monday morning in a public, family-friendly place.

I have more opinions about the "judgmental card," but for now, allow me to say I believe I have every right to be judgmental when it comes to my children. Yes, I should be able to *judge* what they are exposed to, and they should *never* be exposed to sexually graphic content and expletives in a vehicle maintenance department or at a community ball field.

A wonderfully wise friend defended my stance this way: "Why do you think movies are rated based on the language, violence, and nudity? Why do you think books and magazines containing nudity and sexually graphic images are not in the checkout lane at your local Walmart or grocery store? *Most* parents I know try to protect their kids from these images and from foul language. I don't see that as judgmental, but rather *good* judgment on the part of the parent."

The thing is, *all judgment isn't bad*. It's incredibly sad that this has become a foreign concept.

I have the right to be disgusted at your inappropriate clothing and lack of morals.

I have the right to shield my children from your perversion.

I have the right to withhold my respect for you on the basis of your disrespectful acts.

I have the right to judge you if you give me a valid reason to do so.

I also have the right to believe that too many people in our society have no common sense. They remind me of my German shepherd / Labrador mix, Ella. (I love her to pieces, but she doesn't have the sense God gave a fly.) She runs right in front of my car every time I pull down the driveway. Thankfully, we live far off a country road that doesn't get much traffic, so I don't worry about her getting hit by anyone

> The thing is, *all judgment isn't bad*. It's incredibly sad that this has become a foreign concept.

but me. But one day that happened. She ran right into the side of my car as I navigated down the drive. I slammed on the brakes when I heard the loud thump. Ella was tipped over in the yard. She was okay, just a little stunned (and her eyes were crossed for a few days), and she hopped back up. Her tail started wagging furiously, and guess what she did? She ran right in front of my car again.

Absolutely no sense whatsoever.

But I think even Ella would have enough sense not to put on a collar that sports the f-word before going to PetSmart.

Inebriated, foul-smelling men at concerts

I'm always seated next to a drunk man with a scorching case of BO. He loves to wave his lighter in the air, sing incorrect lyrics loudly and off-key, and high-five me during every guitar solo while the fumes from his pit hair pelt me in the face.

Chapter Two

Get Over It

In America we're inundated by media influence. Unless we're living under a rock, we cannot escape it. Unfortunately, this also means we cannot avoid the growing number of people who are continually offended—on social media especially. There are folks in an uproar over song lyrics, jokes, tweets, commercials, slang, and all manner of things, including a video of a Southern woman sitting behind the steering wheel of her car telling the story of an obese man who hit her in the face with his stomach.

It happened on a flight out of Memphis. A large man decided to store his carry-on in the compartment right above my seat. Fine. No problem. However, his carry-on didn't quite fit, so he started shoving his bag with force, leaning into it with his full weight over and over again. While he did so his large protruding stomach, which was exposed due to his T-shirt riding up darn near to his nipples, repeatedly hit me in the cranium. I put my hands up to shield myself from the girth and even let out a muffled, "Excuse me, sir." I don't think he heard me beneath the layer of soft flesh that covered my head like a hairy, sweaty hat.

I told that story via video on my social media outlets—because if I get hit in the face with someone's abdomen, I'm going to tell people about it. The backlash started. I don't think I've ever received such hateful feedback in my life. People were offended. They felt the need to defend this man they didn't even know because I dared "make fun" of someone who was "morbidly obese" and probably "had multiple health conditions."

One Facebook user said, "You wouldn't be so mad if a skinny man had his stomach in your face."

I responded, "Ma'am, I am going to lodge a complaint if *any* man has his stomach in my face—excluding my husband, but I don't prefer that either."

I was simply describing what happened. The girth of that man's stomach was the reason for my discomfort. I was telling this story with humor, but I was choosy with my words too. I was not rude and crude and purposefully did not call the gentleman the forbidden f-word.

You know which f-word I'm referring to here. It rhymes with cat, and if you call any person that word, including yourself, "they" say you are body shaming and deserve to be waterboarded.

My family is no stranger to that word. My great-grandmother, Bess, was a large woman. Her daughter, my Granny Rebecca, was her main caregiver and absolutely adored her. However, she wouldn't think twice about saying something like, "Mama, are you getting too fat for that dress? Do I need to buy you some new dresses?" My great-grandmother never once responded, "Rebecca, I'm highly offended at your remarks. How dare you body shame me that way." Heavens no. Bess would answer, "No, I'm not too fat for the dress. Now pass me the mashed potatoes."

My great-grandmother lived to see 103 years on this earth and had seen her share of hardships. She wasn't about to waste one iota of time being offended at the f-word.

As a fat kid, I understood Gran-Gran's lack of offense—and I'm using the f-word to describe myself because that's what I was. I wasn't "big-boned." I was fat as a tick. My Southern mama cooked up home-made biscuits or cornbread and potatoes with every meal. My waistline proved it, and I owned it. I didn't call other fat kids fat, because even though I wasn't offended by the word, I knew it wasn't the nicest one in the world to use. But I called *myself* fat because . . . I was fat.

I may have learned my brand of honesty and sarcasm from one of my all-time favorite shows, *The Golden Girls*. It's true that I know every line to every episode and am a firm believer that it contains some of the greatest sitcom writing ever conceived. Who can deny that Bea Arthur giving Betty White the side-eye is anything other than hysterical? And it's evident that the *Golden Girls* writers and actors didn't care about offending anyone. They freely made fun of one another and anyone else in sight. They weren't afraid to push boundaries. And you know what? I think it's hilarious. But if it were a new sitcom, some woman would surely be clutching her pearls and demanding it be taken off the air because it is "offensive."

I'm personally not offended at a comic who makes fun of white women. *I'm* a white woman. I do things stereotypical white women do.

Most comedy specials I've watched and most comedians I've seen live crack jokes at the expense of others with no regard for race, gender, or social status. Everyone is fair game. I'm personally not offended at a comic who makes fun of white women. *I'm* a white woman. I do things stereotypical white women do. I drive an SUV. I wear monogrammed pullovers. I have lap dogs. I own Birkenstocks. Target is life. It's orthodox, yes, but it's true. And it's funny.

I admit to doing the same at times. One particular example took place in December 2004, back in my party days—before Jesus got ahold of me.

After a long evening of bar hopping and the kind of loud cackling that can only be produced by helium-sucking hyenas and intoxicated twenty-three-year-old girls, my friends and I decided to call it a night. However, we couldn't rest our spinning heads on our pillows without first stopping off at a convenience store for fourth-meal snacks—because nothing is better for a belly full of Jägermeister than a bag of Doritos, a cold can of Dr. Pepper, and fried chicken that's been sitting under a heat lamp for fourteen hours.

My friends made their purchases and went out to the car, leaving me alone in the creepy gas station to be robbed or maimed or whatever happens to drunk, vulnerable girls in creepy gas stations at three in the morning. But I didn't care that I was all alone in the store except for the cashier smoking a Camel and picking stuff out of his beard. I was too busy mulling over critical decisions on the candy bar aisle. Did I feel like a nut or not?

I heard the jingle of the Christmas bells hanging on the convenience-store door and I drowsily looked up to see who was entering the building. When what to my wondering eyes should appear but a miniature person in my dazed fog of liquor and beer.

Yes, he was a little person. But he wasn't just any little person. He was a little person who looked exactly like Lionel Richie.

I suddenly felt starstruck, and the alcohol surging through my veins felt starstruck too. It was so starstruck, in fact, that it headed straight for that part of my brain that signaled my mouth to produce extremely intoxicated starstruck babble. I immediately began having a mental conversation with myself.

Don't say anything. Just don't do it.

But I had to say something. I had to know if this man was aware that he looked just like Lionel Richie.

No, you don't. You're going to offend him in some way. Keep your mouth shut.

I must.

No, you mustn't. You are too intoxicated for this conversation to turn into anything other than a drunken, nonsensical, and highly offensive puddle of vocal diarrhea.

Okay, okay. I won't say anything.

Good girl.

I bit my lip, grabbed a Snickers bar, and walked right past little Richie.

Don't say—

"Excuse me, sir," I said, interrupting my voice of reason.

Well, here we go.

"Yes?" He tilted his head back to look up at me, a whopping five-foot-eleven Amazon woman in black heels.

"Has anyone ever told you that you look just like Lionel Richie?"

"Yes." He laughed. "I hear that often."

Okay, walk away. You've asked your question. He answered. Now just walk away.

I silently nodded at the voice in my head, fully prepared to wish him a good night, head to the checkout counter, and purchase twelve dollars' worth of saturated fat and sugar.

But I couldn't.

Don't—

"Say you, say me," I began singing, right there beneath the flickering florescent lights in a 7-Eleven, to a little person who was the spitting image of Lionel Richie. "Say you're only four foot three."

That. Just. Happened.

I stood there with my mouth open, shocked and ashamed at the lyrics that had just escaped my drunken lips. I glanced over at the clerk behind the counter, and he was so stunned that he'd paused mid–beard pick while the ashes on his cigarette grew. The greasy, chickeny air was suddenly thick with tension, and a woozy elephant stood in the store. That elephant was me.

I expected this small man, with his impeccably groomed mustache and perfectly picked afro, to really let me have it. I expected him to throw the quart of motor oil that he held in his hands at my face. I expected him to climb me like a six-foot-tall tree reeking of Seagram's Seven and punch me in my smeared raccoon eye. I expected him to verbally let me know he was offended and point out what a horrible and politically incorrect idiot I was.

But instead, without missing a beat, he gave a little smile and sang right back to me, to the tune of "Dancing on the Ceiling"

"Tall drunk girl, what a feeling. You can reach the ceiling."

I was suddenly more starstruck than ever.

I was starstruck because I'd just met the coolest little-person-Lionel-Richie lookalike to ever purchase motor oil in a 7-Eleven at three in the morning. We had sung our own versions of Lionel Richie songs to each other. And for the clerk, those were some sweet sounds coming down on the night shift.

Lionel Richie did not seem offended at my idiocy. He went with the flow. He dished it right back to me. He laughed with me. He was easy like Sunday morning.

Lines can certainly be crossed. I do find it offensive when someone mocks my Lord or hurts my children in some way. If you have any common sense, you can probably discern what I'm addressing in this chapter. I am in no way condoning bullying or abuse; however, there are more important things in this life than getting outraged over the lyrics to an innocent Christmas song and making mountains out of every little molehill.

Until I became popular on Facebook, I had no idea people found such offense over jokes and sarcasm. I grew up in a household where one-liners and digs at each other were common and even welcomed. My children still do that. They will "burn" each other with insults. They do the "You're so stupid . . ." jokes and the "Your mama is so dumb . . ." jokes (which makes no sense because they have the same mother—and that mother is me). They dish it out, *and* they can take it. It was the same when I was growing up. I guess I naively thought that everyone was raised this way. I thought everyone had seen Eddie Murphy's *Raw*. I thought everyone enjoyed a good dose of comedy and "roasting."

I quickly learned I was wrong.

The "body shaming" video I made about the obese man at Memphis International wasn't the first time I realized how sensitive people are. People will comment on jokes or videos I've posted and come up with grievances that I would never have considered in a million years—outlandish claims that I am intolerant or racist or narrow-minded. I've even been scolded for making fun of myself. If I can't make fun of myself, who can I make fun of?

It must be awful hard to live in this world when you are offended all of the time. How can you even turn on the radio or watch a television show or scroll through Instagram photos if you are constantly on the defensive? It seems like such a rigid, hard way to live—searching for controversy where there is none. With your face in a scowl while you spew an angry twelve-hundred-word comment on someone's Facebook post that was meant to summon a little laughter, not outrage.

If ever I do come across an article on the internet that I find offensive, I know my comment isn't going to change the author's mind. It's simply a waste of time for me to furiously pound on my keyboard. Often it is necessary to stand up for what you believe in, but a comment section isn't the place to do that. It's highly in-effective. I know. Anytime someone leaves me a negative comment or e-mail (please stop e-mailing me; I will never reply to anyone who begins an e-mail with the words "Look here . . ."), it doesn't faze me in the slightest. Never has my mind been changed because a woman holding seven cats in her profile picture told me I was wrong.

There is a particular television show that I loathe. Anytime

I've seen it, the characters are mocking Jesus and Christianity. I think it's vile. Profane. Immoral. Blasphemous. Do you know how I handle my abhorrence for this show? *I don't watch it.* Isn't that genius?

Think about what offends you. You have every right to be insulted. You really do. However, how do you handle it? One of my favorite pastors, Adrian Rodgers, once said, "When someone offends you, you're given the opportunity to show Jesus." Does your offense really matter in the grand scheme of things? Can you look past what a certain person believes and respect him or her anyway? Is it worth protesting? And if it is worth protesting—if it is something you value and hold dear to your heart—do you protest it peaceably and with some common sense, or do you parade around like an irate fool? You'll never be taken seriously, by me at least, if you march with a picket sign, wearing a bodysuit that looks like a vagina.

Oh mercy. I'm sure that offended someone.

Doctors-in-training observing my pelvic exam

When the gynecologist asks if some students can watch my examination, I want to ask, "May I bring some friends over to watch you sit on the toilet, doctor? No? Then, no."

Chapter Three
Detours and Differences

You've heard that men are from Mars and women are from Venus, and I have learned it's true—if Mars is a place where pooping takes forty-five minutes and asking for instructions or directions is considered unnecessary. Jason was my first steady boyfriend, and we hadn't been dating very long when I realized just how different the genders are.

Hours after we were married in 2005, we were scheduled to fly from Nashville to Florida where we would board a Royal Caribbean cruise to Nassau, Bahamas. There was an issue with our "buddy passes" that my airplane pilot brother-in-law reserved for us, so we instead had to drive thirteen hours down to Cape Canaveral, where the ship was departing.

Because I am extremely compulsive about preparation, this change in plans had me in a panic. I did the math and knew we would be pushing it if we drove all the way down to the cape.

Jason, however, was excited about being on the road for so many hours. He was excited we were already doing something "adventurous" and "spur of the moment" on our first day of matrimony.

After some convincing on his part, I began to look forward to our trip. It would be like a Hallmark movie—newlyweds on the open road with shoe-polish wedding bells drawn on the back glass of my Jeep to prompt all of I-40 to wave and honk horns. Jason and I would talk about our future, giggle at each other's jokes, hold hands, and listen to soft-rock radio. Oh, and I would use the time to write thank-you notes to everyone who had brought gifts to our wedding and shower.

So we dropped off my beloved Lhasa apso, Peaches, at my mother's house and began our long journey to Cape Canaveral. Jason reasoned that we'd both been to Florida enough times in our lives to find our way without the help of a MapQuest printout or a good old Rand McNally in the glove compartment. (Oh, the good old days before smartphones.)

"We just take the interstate and then another interstate, and as long as we keep heading south, we will eventually end up at the ocean" is not very logical to a woman, but apparently it makes perfect sense to a man.

We did finally hit the ocean after sixteen hours of wrong turns. We listened to the entire Alabama box set twice and were so tired we had to stop for a few hours of sleep at a roach motel in Podunk, Georgia, which wasn't even on the way to Cape Canaveral, Florida. There was no giggling or hand holding involved. In fact, it was more like a Griswold family road trip. I was sure that our future together would consist of driving confusedly around the Sunshine State for the rest of our lives until we finally got tired of traveling and were forced to live on an airboat in the Everglades.

"But we got here on time, right?" Jason refuted my argument as we rushed to board the ship moments before it left the dock.

"Yes," I said, "but we still had to spend our first night of marital bliss arguing in a smelly hotel with crime-scene tape in the parking lot."

Several years later Jason was required to put together a swing set for our daughter's third birthday. For some reason he refused to read the instructions. Hours of frustration and flying expletives followed, and we ended up with a squeaky slide and extra screws.

"But it got built, didn't it?" Jason refuted my argument as little Natalie giggled and slid down the slide.

"Yes," I said, "but are crickets being tormented back here, or is that the swings?"

(In his defense, that swing set held up beautifully and provided years of enjoyment to our children and their friends.)

They say if your marriage can survive building a house, it can survive anything. In 2017 we put that to the test and began construction on our dream home, nestled on seventy acres of Tennessee's most beautiful woodland. In those ten months (307 days, to be exact), Jason and I spent a lot of time together. We spent a lot of time seeing things *differently*. He was unsure about my choice of doorknobs and paint colors and ceiling fans. He couldn't see my vision and thought I was using so many gray tones that living in that house would be like living inside a nimbostratus cloud. Then he sent me down to Lowe's, assuming I could just walk in and find a fourteen-inch diameter electric gable vent fan, and he couldn't understand what was wrong with me when I came home empty-handed. And then, when I picked out two completely different tones of white for our exterior brick, he couldn't see the difference.

That experience taught me yet again how different the two of us are. But I was incredibly proud when Jason relented and trusted me enough to give me full control of the aesthetics. At the end of the building process, he sat on the couch and looked around our beautiful (gray) living room and said, "You did a fine job, Susannah."

Never in my life would I hop in a car and drive sixteen hours without a map or a full tank of gas. I read and reread and re-reread instructions before I assemble anything. I have made Easy Mac over a million times in my life, but I still pull the box from the garbage to make sure I'm adding enough butter and milk. I just don't like to fly by the seat of my pants. But Jason doesn't mind doing that at all. He'll wing something in a heartbeat, saying, "It's all good. Why are you so concerned, Susannah? Why are you planning the route five days before we are set to leave? Why are you so stressed?"

Not surprisingly, our parenting styles are different as well. I prefer that our children don't run in the yard barefoot during a lightning storm or wear church clothes in the mud, but Jason says they're all right. He'll enforce legit rules to keep our children protected, such as wearing helmets when riding ATVs and knowing how to safely operate a deer rifle, but he certainly doesn't sweat the small stuff the way I do. He's usually asleep for over an hour every night while I'm still wide-eyed, staring at the ceiling, fretting about everything from the stains on Natalie's white softball pants to the last time Bennett brushed his teeth.

(For what it's worth, Natalie and Bennett are turning out to be opposites, just like their parents. She schedules things on her calendar far in advance. She is a planner, an organizer, a note taker. He doesn't know his own birthday is tomorrow.)

Although Jason does things differently than I do, he still manages to get them done. Mostly. No matter how hard I try, I can't get my head around the idea that pulling melted Tupperware from my dishwasher and putting it in the wrong cupboard is "getting things done." But Jason does, and I am learning not to yell about it (as much). Just as he let me pick out the brick for our home, I have to let him do some things his way.

All this has been a learning process for me. Several years ago I was ranting and raving about my marriage online. I meant for my sarcasm about Jason to be humorous and harmless, but I eventually had to admit it could be detrimental to our relationship. This conviction led me to write an article about mistakes I make as a wife. It was shared over a million times and was one of my most controversial posts to date.

In that post I owned up to my lack of respect for Jason, including the constant jokes at his expense, my always looking like a bum when he got home from work, forgetting his lovey-dovey needs. (I refuse to say sexual needs. My mother-in-law is reading this book.) And especially the sin of putting my children ahead of him.

And yes, I said sin.

You see, when Natalie Ann was born, she became my reason for living. When Bennett came into this world four years later, he joined his precious sister on her pedestal. For a long time their happiness and care superseded my husband's happiness and well-being. It was easy for me to neglect Jason because I was so preoccupied with our children. It was too easy to get wrapped up in ball practices and extracurricular activities, hauling kids all over town. I found it far too easy to forget that, according to God's Word, we should only love Him more than we love each other. The Bible doesn't say our children come third, but it does say a husband and wife are one flesh, so it stands to reason that children are third in familial relationship priorities.

While jokes about marriage are as old as time and Jason laughs when I grumble about his constant flatulence or the way he chews so loudly I think his jaw is going to crack, I am guilty of taking it too far. I'm guilty of forgetting that, as his wife, I am meant to encourage him, pray for him, support him, and even compliment him. He is a wonderful husband, father, and provider who deserves that and so much more.

I also think Jason deserves my efforts to look nice for him. This may strike you as way too 1950s—if so, you're not alone!—but good gracious, don't we wives need to put forth some effort?

Now, I am in no way saying a woman should put on full-face makeup and greet her husband in nothing but Saran Wrap and stilettos when he comes home from work every afternoon. I have even sent Jason text messages like this: "Let me know what time you'll be home so I can get out of my pajamas and appear to have been productive today." Many days, brushing my teeth and popping the zit on my chin is the extent of my beauty regimen.

I'm thirty-three weeks pregnant as I write this, and I cannot deny that during this pregnancy, I could often be found in a sweatshirt with bacon-grease stains and four-dollar leggings from Walmart. And I know, without a doubt, that Jason loves me anyway. He looks at me standing there in the bathroom in a Turbie Twist while plucking my chin hairs and thinks I'm still the most beautiful woman he's ever seen. (That's what he says anyway.)

However, I won't deny how good it feels when Jason compliments me after I've cleaned up, put on deodorant, and accessorized with scarves and my "sparkly danglies" (earrings). And I know it makes him feel good that I make the effort for him.

Inner beauty is a wonderful, pure, lovely, noble thing. Proverbs 31 describes a beautiful woman clothed with strength and dignity. But there's nothing wrong with removing eye boogers and flossing your teeth for your husband.

> **Proverbs 31 describes a beautiful woman clothed with strength and dignity. But there's nothing wrong with removing eye boogers and flossing your teeth for your husband.**

I also believe that once my teeth are flossed at night, I can't necessarily go straight to sleep. Listen, I'm tired. I'm tired a lot. By 9:00 p.m., I'm worn slap-out. And I still have to fold laundry, pack lunches, load the dishwasher, check my e-mail, make a grocery list, take the dogs outside to potty, lock all the doors, turn off all the inside lights, and turn on all the outside lights. The last thing I want to do is play birds and bees. But good golly, men need that. They need it as much as the dogs need to potty. That's how God wired them, and as wives we have to respect that.

This in particular is what caused such controversy when I posted my confession online. I was accused of being a doormat and counseling other wives to be doormats too. But never did I suggest that a woman ought to roll onto her back like a submissive dog every time her husband scratches her belly.

What I did say was we shouldn't be so selfish as to neglect our husbands' needs. If we have a loving, faithful, respectful husband, he deserves our intimacy. And of course, that means he's also going to be the kind of man who respects us and backs off when we are tired or sick or overwhelmed and need some precious sleep or time alone. I don't know why this is controversial at all, actually.

Jason and I have been different since day one, and we are both guilty of mistakes, but gosh, I love that man. That love is what makes me a better wife today than yesterday. I will still hold that love in my heart when we rock on our porch and watch our grand-children run through the green summer grass. Our love is what will allow him to forgive me when I forget to buy his glucosamine or put tennis balls on his walker.

**THINGS THAT WORK
MY NERVES #10**

Autobiographical recipes

If you post a recipe online, your twelve-paragraph story of
how this dessert has impacted your life isn't required.
Just tell a sister how much butter I need.

Chapter Four

No Thanks to You

I rushed into Bed Bath & Beyond one Saturday afternoon and quickly printed off a wedding registry. The wedding was only a few hours away, and I was about to pay for my procrastination—literally, because all of the inexpensive gifts had been purchased. Since the spatulas and napkin rings were already bought, what was left? A cordless vacuum cleaner that cost more than a fully loaded Kia and luxurious, king-sized, twelve-hundred-thread-count sheets that made me question whether my bedclothes were made of parchment paper.

Because I am frugal (read: cheap), I opted to simply purchase a fifty-dollar gift card. I liked the couple all right, but not well enough to fork over hundreds for them. Between you and me, because they couldn't remain boyfriend/girlfriend for more than three months at a time without breaking up (according to their posts on social media), I didn't foresee them being married more than a year. That high-end vacuum cleaner would probably end up in a yard sale. (I was wrong. They are still married. God is good.)

I took the gift card home, and my husband and I got all spiffed up in our "going out" clothes. We dropped the children off at their grandmother's house and headed to the church for the elegant evening wedding. The bridesmaids were lovely, as were the flowers and music and the candlelight ceremony. It was a very upscale event, and I was not surprised that the bride had registered for premium Egyptian cotton. To sleep on anything less than twelve hundred thread count would be considered sackcloth sacrilege.

At the reception I placed the BB&B card on the gift table. I then moved it about twelve more times to save it from falling to the floor and being swept up with the trash after some drunk guest bumped into the table during "Brick House." That kind of thing gives me extreme concern. I know it stems from accidentally throwing away a fifty-dollar bill my grandmother gave me on my sixteenth birthday. I had a full-fledged anxiety attack over losing that gas and Creed CD money.

Once I finally felt like the card was secure, we ate tenderloin and hors d'oeuvres (yes, I googled how to spell that) and danced to the Commodores. We hugged the young and in-love couple, thanked them for inviting us, drove to pick up our sleepy children, and went home to sleep on our Walmart sheets.

A few weeks passed. And a few more. And the happy bride posted nearly every day on her social-media accounts. She wrote updates about her new hubby and their cute, quaint apartment (that did not require a cordless vacuum because the cord to any vacuum would be longer than their living room). She uploaded 382 photos of the wedding and changed her profile picture every ten minutes. She seemed particularly enamored of the shots of her and her spouse gazing romantically at each other in the middle of a cotton field.

As a born and bred Southerner, I was perplexed. She was on her phone or computer every day, writing love notes and uploading pictures. So why hadn't she composed even a quick e-mail of thanks for our gift? Had she thanked anyone for those knickknacks to decorate her cozy apartment and casserole dishes to hold the Hamburger Helper she so lovingly prepared each night for her beloved? She obviously had the time, what with the twelve-paragraph status updates describing how blessed she was to roll over on sheets that felt like butter every morning and gaze at the man of her dreams.

I wrote thank-you notes in the car—on the way to the departure point for our honeymoon cruise—a few hours after I said "I do." Maybe that was a tad extreme, but I knew life would be hectic when Jason and I returned home, and the importance of getting those suckers out in a timely manner was part of my DNA. I wouldn't dare let Mrs. Martha or my husband's grandmother forget how appreciative I was of their love, support, and Pyrex.

I also addressed little blue and pink notes while my babies still had thrush and cradle cap. I knew how expensive butt paste and high chairs were. Thanking people for their gifts and for making me feel so special and loved throughout my pregnancies was as important as feeding those newborns of mine, who needed to eat more often than a grizzly bear on steroids.

That's just how we operate in the South. We are raised to say "yes ma'am" and "no ma'am" and smile kindly and curtsy. Well, maybe no one curtsies anymore, but if I didn't say "yes ma'am" or "no ma'am" and my mother or grandmother heard me, I got whopped upside the head with whatever was in hand—including but not limited to purses, Bibles, ladles, and to-go boxes containing spaghetti.

> If I didn't say "yes ma'am" or "no ma'am" and my mother or grandmother heard me, I got whopped upside the head with whatever was in hand—including but not limited to purses, Bibles, ladles, and to-go boxes containing spaghetti.

When a bride or new mother who was raised in the South doesn't send a note or, heck, at least an e-mail or a text, she should know better. If she was raised by Southern women, then they would've smacked her upside the head if she didn't use her manners. She would've had a Bible-toting grandmother who told her that the Good Book instructs us to give thanks in all circumstances. Not saying thank you is just rude and self-centered in the South.

When I worked a temp job many years ago and didn't make much money, I still scrounged enough together to buy a deviled-egg carrier for a wedding shower. That particular kitchen item may not seem like much, but they come in real handy when you're asked to bring the eggs to a family function. You can't just pile deviled (stuffed) eggs into a Tupperware container or casserole dish. If you do the eggs tip over, and you end up with a messy yolk and paprika conglomeration. A nice, reliable deviled-egg carrier is a true staple of every Southern kitchen.

Anyway, that bride-to-be never sent me a note or even said, "Thank you, Susannah."

Let's fast-forward more than a decade. That couple has gone on to have three children. They have diapered butts, cleaned up spills, scrubbed crayons from the walls, bought prom dresses, and probably carried hundreds of stuffed eggs to and fro in that carrier. And yet they never once told me thank you. Their oldest just graduated high school, and I sure hope they enjoyed that case of diapers I bought for him eighteen years ago, but I don't really know because they never thanked me for them. (For the record, I never received a thank you for the BB&B gift card either.)

This issue isn't just about wedding presents, of course. What about people in the public sector? Why do I tell cashiers thank you after I've handed them money for gasoline or fast food, but they don't say a word in return? They don't even crack a smile. Shouldn't they be thanking *me*?

Just once I'd like to hear, "Thank you, dear customer, for getting your fuel from this station instead of the one across the street."

Gratitude and manners are definitely learned skills, especially in this area, and I'm here to help. How about, "Thank you for helping to keep this service station open, therefore providing me with a paycheck, a roof over my head, and clothes on my back"?

Or "Thank you, ma'am, for shopping at our store, although you knew you would get stuck behind an incredibly slow-walking grown woman in *Toy Story* pajama pants while you were simply trying to purchase laundry detergent."

Or "Thank you for waiting in this fast-food line for twenty minutes, only to receive cold french fries. Your patronage affords me luxuries like electricity and water."

And can I at least get a little wave from the woman I just let cut in front of me in the school carpool line? Just a little wave. Not a big one. You don't even have to use all five fingers. Just the first finger will suffice, maybe with a little nod. I mean, I did not have to let you cut in front of me. But now that I have, I totally regret it and feel like plowing into the rear of your van to crush the stick-figure family on your back glass. I won't do it though—because I was raised to have manners.

Maybe I'm expecting too much. Maybe it's absurd that I've been known to tell a person thank you for a thank-you note, but since I get one so rarely these days, I really appreciate it when I do. Being grateful and showing your thanks is an awesome attribute. I hold manners and politeness to a high standard. But you know what? Manners were God's idea. He tells us to do unto others. He's the author of love and kindness. And I'm proud to pass these manners and morals on to my children.

If my kids come to your door on Halloween, little Mario and Princess Peach will thank you for those Skittles. If you purchase cookie dough or popcorn or magazines or candles or take out a second mortgage to help support their school, they will thank you. If their friends' parents give them a ride or pay for their food or invite them over, they'd better thank them. And if they don't, please let me know and I'll impart my Southern upbringing to them. They will get a whack upside the head with whatever is in my hand, including but not limited to a purse, Bible, ladle, or to-go box containing spaghetti.

I remember a little girl who came to my daughter's birthday party many years ago. She was the only child who didn't thank me when I handed her a Little Mermaid paper plate topped with chocolate cake and ice cream. Instead she grabbed that dessert from my hands with kind of a snotty, bratty look on her face and then proceeded to wipe brown icing all over my favorite patio chair. And a few minutes later, she tugged on my shirt and said, "Susannah, I want another piece."

Um, what? Did a five-year-old really just call me by my first name and demand another piece of cake without saying please? In the South, children either say "Miss" or "Mister" before using the first name of an adult. So when that precious child spoke to me, I had to sit hard on the inclination to have a full-fledged come-apart on that kid. But I realized she hadn't come into this world demanding chocolate and calling adults by first names. She'd been taught that—or had never been taught good ol' Southern manners. And I will be darned if my children will act so disrespectfully. (Needless to say, she wasn't invited to our home again.)

If you thank people who have done something nice for you (and you do not have to be a new mother or bride-to-be to do so), then I would like to thank you. Thank you for showing appreciation. Thank you for thinking of others. Thank you for doing unto others. Thank you for making this world a brighter place.

Now say, "You're welcome."

People who point out how Southern I am

I was born and raised in the South, and I say "y'all"—but that doesn't mean I'm an uneducated hillbilly who has been engaged to a distant cousin and has a moonshine still in the woods behind my home.

Chapter Five

Act Your Age, Not Your Shoe Size

There were multiple times in elementary school when a certain friend of mine caught an extreme case of the bossies. When I wanted us to climb the monkey bars together, she insisted we swing—and if we didn't swing, she insisted our friendship was over. I vowed right then I was done with her dominant behavior. I was so serious about it that I refused to sit with her at lunch. Instead, I ate my beef stroganoff with another eight-year-old girl and talked about what a bossy pants my ex-friend was. I swore I would never play with her or invite her to spend the night again. All she did when she came over was tell me what toys to play with in my own house anyway.

Then I got to high school and discovered "real" arguments with girlfriends where lies were told and secrets were spilled. I concealed my hurt and found consolation in other girls, who would join me in bashing whichever awful, no-good friend I happened to be at odds with.

I hate to admit it, but there were plenty of situations when I was the awful, no-good friend. I whispered about passersby in the hallway for no valid reason. The girl with the flawless skin and the new car who dated my crush was my mortal enemy. The jealousy bubbling inside of me, with my awkwardly tall frame and bangs in the shape of a curling iron, turned into hatred. I repeated hearsay as if it were fact, hoping the person listening to my gossip would repeat it also. I spread rumors and fanned fires in revenge for wrongs I felt had been committed against me. In my mind, I was back in elementary school, irately checking the "no" box on the note asking if I was still someone's friend.

Thank God I (mostly) matured. I became a grown-up. And I thought the people around me were growing up too. I just assumed all women over the age of thirty would talk solely about things like the third-row seat in their SUVs and Paw Patrol on Ice and nontoxic eye cream. I thought mature mothers would be gentle and kind and forgiving of faults. I had no idea that a housewife who makes the best Bundt cake this side of the Mississippi can be as malicious as a sixteen-year-old girl who just caught her boyfriend with another girl at a Taylor Swift concert.

Sadly, I've learned. I'm now almost forty and am a regular witness to junior high–level spitefulness from supposed grown-ups. I hear it in the bleachers at my children's ball games. I read it in texts. I see catty remarks on Facebook.

I'm going to put myself on the hook though. Even though I've matured and am not nearly as hateful as I was in school (those who went to school with me are throwing up praise hands), I am still guilty of speaking unkindness when someone has treated me ugly or when I encounter another mom who seems to have it all together while I just gave my son a spit bath and Febreze'd him before sending him to school.

We all do this from time to time. And why? I believe it happens when we feel wronged or threatened by another woman. We turn into that teenage girl in overalls and Birkenstocks, and we vent our grievances to anyone who will listen because we crave justification. We want someone on our side. We want to feel heard. We don't want to be alone in our hurt or anger.

When I was about thirty, I was crushed by a friend who talked awful about me to a mutual friend. When I learned the things she had said, I immediately sent her a text that would've given my preacher just cause to throw me out of the church. I used every four-letter word I knew and even some five-letter ones. I wasn't about to eat my beef stroganoff with that traitor anymore. She was dead to me.

As soon as I sent the text, I sent out three more to mutual friends, explaining what had transpired between us. I wanted them to know what she'd said about me and how I had responded. Then I waited on their responses to back me up and corroborate that my behavior was acceptable. And of course, that's exactly what they did.

Weeks passed, and I began to feel remorse for the way I had handled the situation. I was too old and used too much eye cream to play the mean girl. Instead of sending out a text that would make George Carlin roll over in his grave, I should have talked to her in person. Or simply cut ties with her and kept my stupid mouth shut.

I prayed about the situation and promised myself I would refrain from being catty like that again. My behavior certainly wasn't pleasing to God or a testimony of my faith. So I decided that from there on out I would practice self-control instead of lashing out without thinking. I was going to act my age, not my shoe size (although my shoe size brings me closer to legal age than I like to admit).

And yet I'm a mere mortal who is sinful to the core. When a girlfriend and I went to dinner one evening several months later, an acquaintance with a slender waistline, glowing skin, and healthy, non-split-end-having hair walked in. She quietly said hello and nodded before disappearing to the back of the restaurant. Her perfume was still lingering in the air when my friend said, "Girrrrlll!"

"What?" I leaned in, eager for her to dish.

We proceeded to talk for fifteen minutes about the woman's recent divorce, which neither one of us had any intimate knowledge of. All we knew was what so-and-so told so-and-so at the PTO meeting. The conversation morphed from her failed marriage to rumors of her son's rebellious behavior and her plan to get breast implants and how she'd gone buck wild since the separation from her husband. On the ride back home, I felt exhausted from the chit-chat, and those familiar waves of guilt flooded me.

I had talked about this acquaintance as if she were my nemesis, but she had never done a hurtful thing to me. We'd only smiled and nodded when we passed each other in the grocery store. And yet my friend and I had critiqued and picked apart every detail of her life that evening. We'd based every opinion of her on hearsay—and jealousy over her twenty-nine-inch waistline.

I felt bad about my part in the demeaning conversation, so in an attempt to somehow redeem my terrible behavior, I sent my friend a text and told her how convicted I was feeling. She responded that she felt the same way, and we concluded that our belittling behavior was rooted not only in jealousy at her ability to wear cute jumpsuits without looking like Michael Myers, but also in feelings of superiority. We looked down on her because our husbands were still with us and we had good kids and we didn't feel the need to get breast implants or party every weekend.

That realization was quite the epiphany for me. Isn't it true, more often than not, that we only gossip about other women that way if we are envious of them or if we want to feel better than them, giving ourselves a pat on the back?

As the mother of girls, I am sickened at the thought of anyone speaking about my daughters the way I've spoken about others. I deserve a million punches in the throat—dating all the way back to elementary school, when I wrote off a friend because she liked Jonathan from New Kids on the Block too. (Why did she have to like Jonathan? I liked him first. Couldn't she be a true friend and pick Jordan?)

I know I'm not alone.

You. Yes, you, reading this right now. I'm willing to bet your ears have perked up at the whisper of gossip. Sometime in your past, you've sneered in jealousy at the woman who used wet shampoo that morning instead of dry. You have sent texts inquiring about things that aren't your business—a cheating husband, bankruptcy, or similar hard times. You've been guilty of tearing a woman down instead of lifting her up. You've behaved like a little brat in pigtails or a pubescent girl smacking gum and flicking her hair over her shoulder. You've felt conviction for your words, your thoughts, your actions, but temptation always seems to creep back in at the first opportunity to flap your tongue.

> Isn't it true, more often than not, that we only gossip about other women that way if we are envious of them or if we want to feel better than them, giving ourselves a pat on the back?

Maybe you're like me, and you like to think that conviction counts for something. The fact that I feel some sort of remorse for being a chatty Cathy is a good thing, right? Surely it means that the Lord is still working on me. That deep down, I'm a decent person. That I know right from wrong. So I vow to start sowing seeds of love instead of seeds of contempt. I promise myself I'll do better.

Then I think about those women who feel no conviction. You know, those women who delight in destructive conversation without any regret. They can't go ten minutes without tearing someone down. They are the ones to watch out for, aren't they? They are dangerous. Truly vindictive. Bitter. Nasty.

There's one woman I know like that. She is so miserable with her own life that she only finds joy in talking negatively about others. Every time I see her coming, I dodge her. She will smile at you or write words of friendship and encouragement on your Facebook wall, but then talk about you behind your back. I don't know how her poor husband puts up with her—

Oh me. There I go. Lord, I apologize.

THINGS THAT WORK
MY NERVES #29

Parents who bring their sick children to school

I understand the grandparents can't babysit because they went to Branson to see Pam Tillis, but school is no place for sick kids. If your child is hugging the porcelain throne, please keep her at home.

Chapter Six

Catch a Bubble and Pray

In the South there are several topics about which people should always think long and hard before they speak—religion, politics, and their favorite SEC football team. These subjects are known to ruin Thanksgiving dinners, end friendships, and incite heated arguments and/or arson.

I stand firm and unwavering in my personal opinions concerning all three, but I am learning not to shove my principles down others' throats or direct name calling and malicious insults to those who do not agree with me. Now I attempt to share my views in a loving, caring way, and if I feel my blood pressure rising to dangerous heights, I simply walk away. That is, I walk away, I repeat the verse in Ephesians that instructs us not to let anger control us, and I may or may not punch the first pillow I find.

As C. J., one of the sweet sixth-grade girls I teach in Sunday school, once told me, "Mrs. Susannah, when you know you need to keep your mouth shut, pretend to catch a bubble and just pray. Like this." Her cheeks puffed out, full of air, as she pretended to hold a big bubble in her mouth.

I once witnessed a fiery quarrel concerning football in a sporting goods store's parking lot. It was apparent the two individuals didn't know each other personally, but their apparel gave clues as to which team they had rooted for in the SEC game earlier that day. I'm not sure how the tiff started, but before I made it to my car on the opposite side of the lot, I heard derogatory language that would make a sailor blush. Expletives were used to describe both team's coaches and quarterbacks. The men kept arguing while their significant others pulled on their arms and jerseys and whined, "Baby, stop."

All I could do was shake my head and sigh. I understand football is its own religion in the South, but I don't think the team you root for or the colors you wear will have any bearing on the state of your soul when you die. The wolf will one day dwell with the lamb, and surely the Tennessee fan will one day dwell with the Alabama fan.

Nothing compares to the angst that comes with politics though. I refrain from revealing my political views on my social-media platforms and blog, although I do care deeply about policy and have staunch beliefs when it comes to voting for government officials. My mother, God rest her soul, was not as quiet about her political stance.

> ✦ **The wolf will one day dwell with the lamb, and surely the Tennessee fan will one day dwell with the Alabama fan.** ✦

Yes, she was one of those retired women who spent her days on Facebook sharing every meme and political story she could find. The bigwigs at Facebook put her in "Facebook jail" and temporarily deactivated her account for brazenly voicing her opinion during a political scandal, which only fueled her fire and inspired her to send e-mails with the subject "Facebook Is Trying to Silence Me" to everyone in her contact list.

Not long after that fiasco, she called me, extremely paranoid, and said "FBI Surveillance Van" kept appearing on her Wi-Fi choices. She was sure the feds were out to get her. Before telling her that a neighbor had named their Wi-Fi that as a joke, I messed with her head a little bit.

"Mama, run to the window. What do you see?"

"There's a landscaping truck across the street. A man is mowing Mrs. Larsen's yard."

"Is he wearing a headset? Like the secret service?"

"I don't think so. He is wearing dark sunglasses though."

"Mama, you need to get out of there. The president is on to you. He knows you've been bashing him on Facebook."

After she passed away in September 2015, I turned on the television in her bedroom for the first time and saw the twenty-four-hour news channel she always watched. It's probably what killed her—her blood pressure spiked to an all-time high watching election coverage, and she died right there in her bed.

I often see people like my mother praise their party or candidate on social media, and no matter how strongly I disagree with them, it is certainly their right to do so. I never write fourteen hate-filled and derogatory paragraphs sentencing them to a fiery eternity. There's no point in that. No one is going to change anyone else's mind or political views because of a Facebook comment. It's just not going to happen. I'll tell you what *will* happen if someone dares to attempt it though: the comments section will turn into an all-out war zone where someone ends up chewing some baby aspirins and someone else posts that GIF of Michael Jackson eating popcorn.

As for religion, the New Testament tells Christians to share the good news of hope and mercy, but stresses that this must be done in love. When Christians protest with signs and slogans that reflect hate instead of love, I imagine it must grieve God's heart terribly.

It is true that our God is a jealous God and even a vengeful God. He hates sin, yes. But we weren't put on this earth to condemn anyone, even if our beliefs do align with the Word of God and theirs do not. Our purpose is to merely be a reflection of Christ right here on earth. We are to sow the seeds of love and let God produce the harvest. Jesus threw over some tables in the temple, but He never paraded around hating those who were lost.

When it comes to sports, politics, and religion, tolerance and open-mindedness are foreign concepts. Instead of just keeping our mouths shut and respectfully agreeing to disagree, we get in an uproar and sever all ties with those who don't see eye to eye with us.

That's our right, I guess. We don't have to hang out with those who don't agree with us. But what if we allow other people's views to steal our joy? What if we stew over another person's opinions so much that it traps us in a state of anger? What if we are so insulted and sickened over a person's views about a certain candidate or team or religion that we cannot even bear to look at them kindly?

Though I loved my mother immensely, I often saw her do just that. She was rarely tolerant of anyone who disagreed with her politically. Mama dubbed anyone an idiot who voted a certain way and then quit inviting them over for coffee.

"Mama, Mrs. Gina hasn't been over lately. Are you two—"

"Gina is an idiot. She voted for _____."

Mama didn't have to agree with Gina. She didn't even have to invite her over for coffee anymore. But Mama made Gina's political stance the burr in her saddle. She gave Gina and her yard sign and bumper sticker too much control over her own emotions.

I remember sitting in a dentist's waiting room with Mama one afternoon when I was a teenager. I thumbed through *Seventeen* magazine and listened to her strike up a conversation with the woman sitting beside her. They talked about a plethora of things that they, as fifty-year-old women, had in common. I could tell my mother was thoroughly enjoying her conversation with this stranger—until the woman said something regarding politics that my mom vehemently disagreed with.

Oh, Lord, I thought.

I quickly shifted my eyes from the magazine to my beautiful, blonde mother sitting in the chair across from me. She became visibly irate—her face turned beet red and her eyes grew wide. I contemplated running to the back of the office and asking the dentist for smelling salts because I just knew she was going to pass out from shock and anger. But before I could sprint from my seat, Mama verbally disagreed with the stranger. The woman fired right back at my mother, and I hid behind the magazine while the receptionist threatened to call the police.

Because I was raised by a woman who sternly believed in certain political views and washed her hands of anyone who didn't believe the same, I've been tempted at times to do the same thing, to cut all ties with friends who have different opinions. These days, I'm finally capable of respectfully disagreeing with others without writing them off.

I won't lie. I have a hard time being tolerant when it comes to certain issues. For example, I believe life starts at conception. The baby girl kicking wildly in my stomach as I write this only reinforces my stance. A true conversation with someone who is pro-abortion is only possible if we know each other well and also respect each other. But I've learned that getting into an argument when that isn't the case will be fruitless and will only stress me out.

So with most people, when issues like these arise, I take a deep breath and change the topic or go to the bathroom to talk to myself in the mirror and rinse my face with cold water. But it takes extreme circumstances for me to cut someone off completely.

One of my dear friends from high school and I no longer speak because she wrote me off for my political and religious beliefs. I didn't know she had unfriended me on social media until I remembered it was her birthday and wanted to post a cake emoji on her wall. She was nowhere to be found in my friends list, so I looked her up and sent her a message to ask why she had dumped me online. Didn't it mean something that we used to share an order of deep-fried pickles at a local fast-food joint after school?

She responded to my message and said she could not disagree more with blog posts I'd written about Jesus, and she was sorely disappointed in my liking certain political posts. She said she didn't need my opinions in her news feed, so she'd given me the heave-ho. Even the happy memories of talking about *Dawson's Creek* over those deep-fried pickles wouldn't sway her.

I was saddened by her message, and I feel bad that she missed out on a cake emoji because of her intolerance. But I'm glad I deliberately put into practice to agree to disagree with people instead of writing them off forever. I've done a pretty good job thus far.

The Bible makes it clear: the response for dealing with conflicting opinions is the same as the preferred response for all circumstances—*love*. Our views shouldn't always be silenced. We are instructed to stand firm in our beliefs in what the Lord says is right, but our stance should always be expressed in love. Whether or not the other party accepts our views, even when they are presented in love, isn't our problem to solve.

I just wish Alabama fans, Democrats, and atheists knew how to express their beliefs in love, but—I'm kidding. Don't be intolerant and toss my book into the Goodwill pile just yet.

**THINGS THAT WORK
MY NERVES #77**

My husband's flatulence

It was funny when we were teens, but two decades
later, if Jason kills one more innocent houseplant
with his methane, I'm changing my Facebook
relationship status to "It's Complicated."

Chapter Seven

Your Screen Time Is Up

When I was a child, we took a road trip to Florida every summer. Those eight hours riding down to the Gulf Coast in the backseat of my mother's champagne-colored (not gold—*champagne!*) Oldsmobile 98 provide some of my fondest memories. I spent the time listening to my Pocket Rocker (Debbie Gibson, no doubt), reading magazines, doing Mad Libs, laughing at my Mad Libs, and writing in my journal. I knew, even at the age of eight, that I wanted to be an author, so I loved to write short stories in spiral notebooks and doodle illustrations to go with them. I never once complained about the long ride. My parents actually complained because I kept sticking my bare feet into the front seat and singing loudly and off-key to "Electric Youth" blasting on my headphones while they tried to listen to their Eagles tape on the cassette deck.

When I spent weekends with my Granny Rebecca, we shelled peas on her porch, took long walks around her neighborhood, played Rook at her kitchen table, drank from Coke cans with Kleenex wrapped around them so they wouldn't sweat, and then watched television together after a home-cooked supper. I loved listening to my grandmother and her neighbors talk about the old days while we sat in her porch swing. I even tagged along to gospel sings at community centers and fire stations and sang "I'll Fly Away" right along with them. It was a special time of learning from and bonding with the older generation.

Once I got my driver's license, I spent Friday nights steering my Mitsubishi Eclipse from Big Star Grocery, around the courthouse, down to the old Walmart parking lot, and back again. And again. And again. I had no way of calling my friends to see where they were. The free weekend minutes on the bag phone plugged into the cigarette lighter didn't kick in until 9:00 p.m. So I just waited until I passed my friends on that strip in the middle of our small Southern town. I'd honk and flash my lights. Then we would pull over in the parking lot next to Sonic to talk and laugh until curfew.

When I went out to eat with my mother and great aunts after church, I listened to their conversations about Aunt Cora's heart palpitations and the newly elected deacons at church. Aunt Cora was the slowest eater on earth, and my food had been fully digested by the time she took the first bite of her biscuit. While waiting for her to shakily and slowly navigate a fork of peas to her mouth, I passed the time by playing that game on the table where you stick pegs in the wooden triangle.

Back in those simpler days, I engaged in face-to-face conversation with family members and friends. I looked out of the car window and pondered the age of trees and the diet of cows. I took in the beauty of old churches and barns covered in rust. If I was ever bored, I found ways to entertain myself. Staring at a screen and negatively affecting my hippocampus was not an option.

Times sure have changed.

Before a life-changing electronics detox that I will tell you more about in a minute, my kids did not know how to ride in the backseat to Nashville (ninety minutes) without being entertained by something that requires a charger. And you could guarantee they were going to fight over the charger at some point. You could also guarantee that at some point I would threaten to throw the device *and* the charger *and* the kids out the window.

Instead of contently listening to what their elders had to say at family functions, those same kids would latch onto a PopSocket and scroll until their thumbs developed a callus. They would rather watch a YouTube video that dumbed them down twenty-five IQ points than listen to a story about their grandparents' hometown in 1965.

I once watched my daughter and her friends sit beside one another on our couch with their screens pressed to their noses. Guess who they were texting? Each other. Instead of turning to speak to the person three feet to her left, Natalie sent that person a text.

How absolutely asinine is that?

And who could I blame but myself?

I was guilty of putting a Leapster in their chubby toddler hands so I could carry on a phone conversation in peace.

When I needed a few minutes to mop the kitchen floor, I plopped them down in a bouncy seat in front of the television and stuck a Baby Einstein DVD into the player. (I thought I was making my kids smart, and I will concede that, thanks to some DVDs, my daughter was spelling her name and identifying all the colors before she knew how to potty.)

I was guilty of buying an iPod for Christmas and a PlayStation for a birthday.

I was guilty of caving to the temptation of peace and quiet by sending my children upstairs to battle on Fortnite.

I often complained they were glued to screens, but a lot of that was my fault.

A friend of my son is eight years old and has never owned a gaming console. He doesn't beg his mother for "fifteen more minutes" of screen time because he's "in the middle of a level." His mom has never flipped the breaker to the game room. Tears have never been shed over video games, and "five more minutes" has never been begged through snotty sobs.

And that's exactly how it should be—but it's not the way it was in our house.

Before we enforced a detox in our home, I would tell my son to get off his iPod and go outside to play basketball, but he would gripe and moan. I would take my daughter's phone every evening before bed and she would make her discontent clear. They would eventually comply with my wishes because I am the mother and they knew that arguing with me never bodes well for them, but their compliance was always grudging.

I just wanted them to know how to appreciate nature and life's simplest pleasures. I wished I had been like my son's friend's mother and never allowed a stupid game console in this house. But how was I to know? Santa had been kind enough to leave a Nintendo under my tree in 1988, and it hadn't been a problem for me. I had never been so obsessed with Mario Bros. that my bike sat on flat tires and covered in cobwebs in the garage for over a year while I discovered warp zones and attempted to rescue Princess Peach. But things were different in our house, especially with eight-year-old Bennett. And especially when it came to gaming.

The main problem was that he didn't know when to quit. He would stay cooped up in his game room for days on end if I allowed it and eventually only come out, with a beard and BO, to use the bathroom. We tried to replace his addiction with sports and music, and although he did enjoy basketball and drum lessons, he would rather be on his PlayStation than do anything else. It was constantly on his mind.

Bennett was also extremely inattentive when a gaming controller was in his hand. I talked with many friends about this. "When he's playing games, he doesn't hear a word I say," I complained. "I tell him to put on his shoes or brush his teeth, and fifteen minutes later he's just sitting in front of the television without shoes on and breath that smells like Post Malone's armpit."

Finally one day Bennett got in trouble for having a nasty attitude, and Jason and I decided, as his punishment, to take away all of his electronics for an undetermined amount of time. No iPod. No PS4. No Nintendo Switch. Our boy flew into a fit of rage. In his anger he said some very disrespectful things to us. When I looked at him, screaming like a lunatic, he didn't look anything like my sweet little boy. He wasn't himself. It scared me to the point of tears.

After only a week without electronics, however, Bennett was a different child. I was so amazed at what I observed in him that I was on fire to share it with the world. I'd expected that the boy would show some change without an iPod in his hand, but I'd had no idea the dramatic improvement that would take place.

Without access to any devices, Bennett was attentive. I asked him to do something one time and he did it. He wasn't preoccupied with thoughts of gaming or too busy searching for his iPod or even so enthralled with a game that he blocked out my voice. He was happier. He was kinder to his sister. He went outside to play without me suggesting that he do so. He did not have a single fit of anger. He read books or drew pictures when he was bored, and he loved it. His teacher said he was more focused. He didn't wake up late for school. He talked more. He looked out the car window and asked questions about trees and clouds and cows. I'd never been so happy to play "I Spy" in my life.

A couple more weeks of detox, and Bennett continued to improve. It was such a "duh" moment for me. I'd always known that too much screen time wasn't good for him, but why hadn't I realized it was the cause of his misbehavior? Maybe not all children are so affected by gaming, but Bennett sure was. Some people can drink. Others become alcoholics. I believe the same principle applies to technology.

Even after we finally allowed Bennett to have his devices back for a weekend, the miraculous change continued. When his screen time was over, he got off the devices without complaint. No begging. No crying. No "Can I finish this level?" or "Fifteen more minutes, Mama, *please*?" He simply turned the power off and found something else to do. No big deal. He did not keep asking when he could play again either. That wasn't even on his mind. When told that from then on he would only have limited screen time—and only on weekends—he did not fall to the floor in a fit of rage. He just nodded and started a conversation about caterpillars and metamorphosis.

> Some people can drink. Others become alcoholics. I believe the same principle applies to technology.

We've stuck with our limits on electronics, and we've seen incredible changes in our son. I've begun putting my phone away more too. I don't want him to see me glued to mine during dinner or while we're sitting together on the front porch after I've told him he's on his entirely too much. And I've had the sweetest conversations and periods of quality time with my daughter, too, since I've cut back on my phone use.

One evening after dinner I put my phone on the kitchen table and went upstairs to Natalie Ann's room. I asked her to put her phone away, too, but when she did it immediately vibrated with a text notification. So I asked her to turn it off. Then we cuddled up in her plush white comforter and talked. We talked about boys and softball and Steph Curry. We talked about our dogs and *The Hunger Games* and Jesus. I heard my phone vibrating on the kitchen table because I'd failed to turn it to silent, but I ignored it. I didn't care what text/e-mail/social-media alert awaited me. I wanted to talk to my little girl.

We played a game of Uno. She beat me. And then we broke out the Old Maid cards that I'd used when playing with my own mother. They are tattered and worn, and the Old Maid has a crease in the corner where some cheater (probably a ten-year-old me) folded it down. When we were finished, she asked me to stay in her room so we could talk some more. So instead of telling her my big, pregnant body longed for my soft bed, I complied. I knew there would be a time when she'd be kicking me out of her room instead of inviting me to stay, so I tried to get as comfortable as possible as she told me more about her friends and who was "dating" in seventh grade.

Later that night I fell asleep and completely forgot about my phone down in the kitchen, glowing and beeping and flashing with alerts. It wasn't until the next morning that I realized how unusual that was—and how much I depend on that device. I might not hold a controller in my hand regularly like my son did, but I depended on that phone to stay connected to the world. When I was done eating dinner, I reached for it. As the DVR fast-forwarded through commercials, I reached for it. Even as I waited at a long red light, I would reach over to reply to a text. When I was talking to my husband and children, I didn't hesitate to mentally leave our conversation when it vibrated to let me know someone or something needed my attention.

When I ignored the phone rattling against the kitchen table downstairs as I really listened to Natalie Ann, it was the first time in a long time I'd done that. I got so much joy watching her laugh until she cried when I told her stories about my childhood. I ran my fingers through her long, blonde hair and prayed with her. She needed my attention more than any e-mail, text, or Facebook notification. And I needed her more than any of those things too.

In Philippians we are told to think on what is noble, pure, and lovely. I had never thought of this verse in terms of gaming and electronics. But for the longest time, Bennett's little brain wasn't thinking on lovely things. He was only thinking about blasting enemies and leveling up. His mind was a garbage dump, and what went in his mind came out of him—out of his mouth and through his attitude and actions.

I want my children to think on those pure, noble things. So when Jason and I were eating dinner at a restaurant last night and saw a baby in an infant carrier—no more than five or six months old—we noticed the mother had her phone strapped to the handle of the car seat. Wide-eyed, the baby silently watched cartoons on the small screen. Mother was able to eat every bite of her dinner and even hold hands with her husband while the couple sitting across from them talked. Jason looked over at me, seven months pregnant (I'm pregnant, not Jason), and he said, "We're not making that mistake again. We're not doing it this time."

I agree with him 100 percent. We're not doing it this time. We're not putting a phone or a LeapPad device or an iPod in the hands of baby number three. I don't want this child distracted by anything but scenery or a good book or conversation. I don't want her to miss watching the deer run across our backyard because she's trying to level up. I don't want a device to be her idol the way it is an idol for so many children . . . and adults.

When she's a little older, maybe . . . in limited doses. The internet and electronics are here to stay, after all. But I've learned that it's a great idea to make disconnecting from outside distractions a priority for my children and for myself as well.

One way I try to do that is by logging out of my social media accounts every few months. I am living my dream as an author, and so much of that success depends on the internet and social media. But sometimes I need time off from both. I need to decompress and focus more attention on my family, my walk with Christ, my hobbies, and the thirsty tomatoes in my garden. Sometimes I just need to take a road trip with nothing for entertainment but conversation, the view out the window, and a stack of Mad Libs.

THINGS THAT WORK
MY NERVES #23

Off-key singers on social media

God has given us all gifts, but He did not give us all the gift
of song. If you can't carry a tune in a bucket, please stop
posting videos of you singing. You aren't channeling your
inner Tammy Wynette, Carla. More like Tammy Why'd-You-
Do-That? And that rendition of Mariah's "Emotions" had me
feeling emotions all right—sadness, disappointment, fear.

You have a purpose, Carla.

This ain't it.

Chapter Eight

You Have Enough Friends

From the ages of eight through thirteen, all I wanted was a four-wheeler. I would watch my friends ride in the field across from our subdivision after school, and I was eaten up with jealousy. So every Christmas and every birthday, I asked for an ATV.

My mama wasn't having it.

You see, my daddy had owned a Big Red three-wheeler and flipped the thing constantly. He would come into the house covered in mud, with a new dent in both the fender and his femur. I promised to be more responsible than Daddy, who was both a daredevil and a drinker, but Mama was adamant: I was not getting an ATV.

Not only did she fear for my safety, but she also argued that ATVs stay broken. Daddy's was always in need of repair (which I'm sure had *nothing* to do with the way he drove the thing) and sat on cinder blocks in the garage for weeks at a stretch. Since my father died when I was eleven (miraculously not from flipping the three-wheeler), we did not have the money to fix one, and my mom didn't know the first thing about ATV mechanics. (I finally got my first four-wheeler at age twenty-seven, when my husband bought it for me. It's on cinder blocks in the garage right now.)

My mama was unwavering on the four-wheeler thing. The fact that it had been the most coveted thing on my wish list every December for years did not mean I was entitled to one. It didn't matter if I kicked and screamed and slammed my bedroom door and blared my Ace of Base CD. It didn't matter that I sprawled out on my bed and screamed into the pillow because I foolishly thought my mother was my enemy.

Though I never got an ATV while I was living at home, I will admit that I was spoiled in other ways. After my daddy died, leaving my mama a widowed single mother who just wanted her youngest child to be happy, she often caved to my pleas. She thought I'd suffered enough watching Daddy fall to the floor one cold November morning and die from a heart attack, so she compensated by allowing me to go to sleepovers even when I was supposed to be grounded for failing my math test. She went from being a stay-at-home mother to working crappy jobs for little pay just to scrounge together enough cash to buy those ripped jeans I wanted.

She wouldn't allow me to have an ATV, but she did put a large down payment from my father's life insurance policy on my first car, a Mitsubishi Eclipse with a sunroof and a turbo power button that didn't do a thing to the engine but let me feel like Dale Earnhardt when I pushed it. Then she told me to get a job to pay for the gas and insurance.

I didn't go without much, in other words. And yet I always knew Mama was the mama. I knew when to shut my mouth and accept "no." She parented the heck out of me, and that's what parents are supposed to do. We should want to raise little people who will go into this big, scary world knowing they aren't guaranteed a thing. We should desire to raise them to go into this world with morals and respect.

I don't want my children to be surprised to discover that responsibility is a given for survival. I don't want to raise slackers who think they can eat Pizza Rolls and play Xbox Live all day instead of clocking in at work. I don't want my children to grow up to be thirty-five-year-old dependents who gripe and moan through life and spend their adulthood on the corduroy couch in the basement.

No, I want to raise professionals. I want to raise successful people who provide for themselves and their future families.

When Bennett was three or four, we made a Target run, and he saw an Avengers toy that he just had to have. Because I don't believe kids deserve thirty-dollar gifts on random Thursdays, I told him no. He fell to the floor in protest, and I was convinced he would be a nominee for Best Actor in a Drama Series at the 2032 Emmy Awards. But I held firm. "You're crazy if you think you get a toy just because we came to Target for paper towels. Get your tail up right this minute and hush your mouth."

> I don't want my children to be surprised to discover that responsibility is a given for survival. I don't want to raise slackers who think they can eat Pizza Rolls and play Xbox Live all day instead of clocking in at work.

Nowadays, as Bennett walks by the toy department, he knows better than to ask for a thing, although he may eye a few items like a recovering alcoholic in a bar. He knows he needs to do some extra stuff on the chore chart or wait until his birthday if he really wants something because otherwise I'm going to tell him no.

Recently, Natalie Ann (overcome with preteen hormones) had the audacity to roll her eyes at me in front of a group of my friends.

Now, that nasty attitude isn't tolerated in our home, and it certainly isn't tolerated in public.

My mother didn't tolerate it from me either. I'll never forget when she turned to me sitting in the passenger seat of her car and chewed me up one side and down another for talking back to her in front of her friends. "You may not agree with what I say, but you wait until we are alone to discuss it with me. Don't you ever disrespect me or tell me I'm wrong in public like that again." I knew my mother meant business, and I never dared argue with her in a group setting again.

I let Natalie know I meant business too. She might not agree with everything I say, but she could not respond to me like I was just one of her friends. I'm not her friend. I love spending time with her. I love laughing with her. I love our inside jokes and secrets. But I'm not a "bestie for the restie" like Kate or Cameryn or Mary. My job isn't to appease Natalie or give in to her every plea or to make her happy all of the time. Sometimes I have to be the bad guy, and I'm okay with that. She might as well get okay with it, too, because that's the way it's going to be.

Growing up, I had a friend whose mother seemed more like one of us kids than an adult. She was young, single, cool, and beautiful. She taught us how to apply eyeliner, and we gossiped over pizza and popcorn. We had no rules at her house. I was allowed to watch PG-13 movies well before I was thirteen. Needless to say, I loved staying the night there, because she was like my friend too.

They moved to another town before we started high school, and it was really no surprise to my mother when we heard that my friend had two children and dropped out of high school and her mom was arrested several times for supplying alcohol to minors.

"That's what happens when you have a friend instead of a mother, Susannah," Mama told me. And she was right. My friend didn't have an adult to tell her no. Her mother even allowed boys to stay the night. I'm positive those children she had at sixteen and seventeen have proved to be blessings to her, but her life sure could have been different had her mother set boundaries.

I'm sure my friend's mother was stressed being a young, single mom. I'm sure she just wanted to have a fun, special relationship with her daughter, and that's the reason she allowed her to run wild. Maybe her own mother was overly strict and she wanted her daughter to have a life she didn't have—freedom to make choices.

My son's addiction to video games was solely my fault because I didn't tell him no. I even used those electronics as babysitters to keep him occupied when I was busy or stressed. And sometimes I caved and refused to tell him no because I just didn't want to deal with the argument that would surely ensue. I wanted to keep the peace. I wanted to be the boy's friend.

No more.

I think every parent wants their children to have what they couldn't, and it's true Natalie Ann and Bennett have been given more opportunities than Jason and I ever had. Jason and I both lost our dads at age eleven and were raised by single mothers. Both of our moms did the best they could for us. They worked to support us and wanted nothing more than for us to be happy, but we were denied things that households with fathers had. I didn't have a daddy to push me to pursue sports, so I gave up on basketball and softball quite easily. It was the same for Jason. Natalie Ann has a daddy to do that—she has a daddy, thank God, to pitch to her in the front yard and play one-on-one in the driveway. His income allows us to play travel ball and go to lessons. That's one thing I didn't have, and I'm so thrilled she does.

Bennett has a daddy to take him to the deer stand and help him replace the spark plugs or flush the carburetor or do whatever needs to be done to get his little youth four-wheeler off the cinder blocks in the garage. He also has a daddy who mowed yards as a boy and worked at a grocery store after school to be able to pay for what he wanted/needed. He has a daddy who has never asked for a handout. He has a daddy who is a wonderful provider and example.

I have to admit, though, that there is one particular way in which I cave and say yes. I purchase those small "fun-sized" bags of chips for my kids' lunchboxes. My mother refused to buy those. Instead, she would buy the big bag of Lays and just put some in small Ziploc bags for my lunchbox because it was so much cheaper that way. I would look over at my friends with their cute little individual bags of Doritos, Fritos, or Cheetos, then look down at my clear plastic bag of crushed chips, and I would vow that one day I would buy my kids the expensive little bags. As God as my witness, even if I had to work two jobs, they would get their fun-sized chip bags.

And they can eat from those fun-sized chip bags while I tell them no.

No, you're not wearing that.

No, you're not going to speak to me that way.

No, you're not going until you've done all of your chores.

No, you're not having a sleepover at the house of someone we hardly know.

No, you're not using your phone right now.

No, you can't go to a Post Malone concert.

No, you aren't skipping practice tonight.

No. No. No.

My kids have enough friends. And darn good parents say no.

**THINGS THAT WORK
MY NERVES #38**

Torturous spa appointments

If I'm bellowing in pain while getting a massage, you're
probably applying too much pressure. This is assault and
battery, Denise. Was Mr. Miyagi your massage instructor?
What's next? A hot towel and a roundhouse
kick to the face?

Chapter Nine

Take Off the Mask

Tell me if you know this woman.

Her Instagram posts leave you nine kinds of jealous. She doesn't even need a filter in her 8:00 a.m. pose with her favorite coffee cup. Meanwhile, you've applied a full face of makeup, but still need to throw on some X-Pro II just so you don't look as pale as Bella on *Twilight*.

Not only does she know everything about scented oil warmers, beaded jewelry, and organic cleaning products, she is authorized to sell it all to you. Her children are salespeople too. They always win the limo ride and the ice cream party because they sold more peaches than the entire state of Georgia could grow. She laminates stuff for fun. She has more Cricut cartridges than you have Tupperware. There's a patent pending on the planner she designed. Her children's birthdays rival anything on Pinterest. Oh, you had a three-tiered cake for your darling's birthday? She had JoJo Siwa fly in.

Maybe she knows how to remove craft paint from the curtains and chili sauce from linen pants. Maybe she gives out samples of a homemade healing lip balm made of honey, cornstarch, and oils. Maybe she can sew drapes and alter pageant dresses and crochet afghans large enough to cover a Chevrolet Suburban. And yet, when you see her in the pharmacy and ask how she's doing, she nearly falls apart as she clings to the prescription for her antianxiety medication. She says the words *busy* and *tired*.

Keeping up appearances is hard work, isn't it?

I'm reminded of a certain Bible story when I see that woman unstrapping a bouncy house from the top of her SUV's luggage rack. In the book of Exodus, our good friend Moses spoke with God for forty days and nights about plans for the tabernacle and the Ten Commandments. When he came down the mountain carrying the two Tablets of Testimony, his face was all aglow because he'd been in the presence of our mighty Creator. Aaron and all the Israelites saw the radiance and were afraid to get close to him at first. But Moses explained the reason for the spark, and I'm sure they thought, "Wow, that Moses sure is blessed. He gets to speak with God and look radiant too!"

Moses covered his face with a veil while in the community and removed it when he went back up Mount Sinai to speak with God again. But while he was wearing that veil, everyone knew he was glowing with God's glory beneath it.

We don't know how long Moses wore that veil, but at some point the shine began to fade. And according to Paul in 2 Corinthians 3:7–18, Moses continued to wear the veil. He didn't want the Israelites to see the glory fade. Maybe he didn't want them to know he was just like them again. Maybe he thought they would think less of him. Whatever his reasons, once the glow was gone, Moses' veil was nothing more than a mask.

Remind you of anyone you know—hiding personal failings and limitations behind a mask of being perfectly competent and put together? To be honest, it reminds me of who I used to be.

I was a people pleaser. I would commit to everything that came my way, kill myself to get it all done, and do my best to make it look easy. I was busier than a moth in a mitten and ended up overwhelmed and on antianxiety medication myself.

Not anymore. I have no desire to be in that place again. So these days what you see is what you get. I'm not afraid to let people know I don't have it all together.

That's not to say I'm like my Aunt Cora who, when asked, "How are you doing?" would honestly answer, "Well, I've been better. My elbow hurts and my ears are ringing and I have two ingrown toenails and I forgot my hair appointment last week so now I have to wait another week before Debbie can see me and the car is making a strange noise and the dog has diarrhea and your Uncle Harvell has diarrhea and I sure hope I don't get diarrhea because . . ." But I don't hesitate to admit I'm no superwoman. I'm perfectly comfortable with saying, "Hey, I will just donate some money to the PTO because my family won't fully commit to selling peaches. We may sell one box to my in-laws, but I'm liable to forget to deliver them to my in-laws, and then we'll just end up with a box of rotten fruit and flies in my garage. Here's fifty bucks instead."

This doesn't mean I've turned into a slacker. I know I have responsibilities and things to do and commitments to keep. But I am not going to wear a mask (or a cape) and pretend to be someone I'm not.

The woman I described above, who portrays perfection online and is cochairing every event in a tricounty radius, might truly love her lifestyle, but I have to believe that level of excellence is only truly possible if you're Jesus—and striving for it can be torturous. Yes, your meatloaf might look like a lump of pink slime compared to her organic bison roll. She might bake everything from scratch and have never popped a can of "that fake frosting" like you have. She might even put banana wheels on motorcycle-shaped sandwiches before she tucks them lovingly inside her son's monogrammed lunch box. But I have to wonder if she ever aims for excellence in . . . resting?

That woman might truly find fulfillment in keeping busy all of the time. Maybe she prides herself on her exceptional homemade fondant, but would she feel like a failure if she packed her children Lunchables once in a while? Does her self-worth depend on her ability to write calligraphy? What if she owned the same printer I do, which can barely put out a black and white letter, much less tie-dyed greeting cards? Would she feel like less of a woman? Less of a wife and mother?

When I see that woman at the pharmacy and overhear her telling the pharmacist her day's schedule before taking the kids to water polo lessons at three, I want to pull her into my arms. I want to say, "Hey, take off that mask. We know you aren't always glowing beneath it, and that's okay."

I mentioned this in my last book, *Can't Make This Stuff Up!*, but it bears repeating. When I was a little girl playing with my Granny Rebecca's makeup, I picked up one of her *Upper Room* pamphlets and turned to a picture that will forever be etched in my mind. Jesus was sitting on the throne with His arms outstretched and a crowd of people at His feet. Moms, dads, grandfathers and grandmothers, even little children—they all bowed down before Him. Some were weeping. Others were sleeping. And below was the scripture from Matthew 11:28, "Come to Me, all who are weary and heavy-laden, and I will give you rest" (NASB).

I was only twelve when I saw that, and I was so burdened at the time with the sudden death of my father that it hit me hard. I envisioned myself in that crowd, resting at the feet of Jesus. And I've gone on to imagine that scene countless times in my life. No mask. No veil. No secrets. No pretending. No busyness. Just me—vulnerable, sinful me—resting at the feet of my Savior.

I'm reminded of the afternoon my precious Malshipoo, Newt, was next to me on the couch. (In case you're wondering, a Malshipoo is a Maltese, shih tzu, and poodle mix. They used to be known as "mutts" but are now called "designer breeds".) While we sat there, Newt kept gnawing at his paw. Several times I reached over to see what was wrong, but he pulled it away from me and started gnawing again. Finally I threatened to feed him dog food for supper instead of a pork chop if he didn't let me see that paw, and he reluctantly let me hold it.

In the bed of his little foot was a cocklebur. I know it must've been painful to start with, but his incessant gnawing had only made things worse. The cocklebur was embedded in layers of wet, slobbery hair and seemed impossible to get out.

"All right, Newt, you're going to have to trust me. Let me help you, okay?"

Newt nodded and crawled into my lap. He rolled onto his back and allowed me to gently pull and unwind the layers of matted hair from the cocklebur. It took a little while, and he flinched in pain several times, but I finally removed it and he licked my cheek as thanks.

> There's relief in surrender. If we would just simply roll over and let God handle it, He will gently unwind and untangle and free us.

As I cooked pork chops that night, I started thinking about our relationship with God and how it relates to that cocklebur story. We get ourselves in a bind and keep gnawing at the problem. We think we really can do it on our own—we can fix that misunderstanding or we can carve 120 pumpkins for the fall fest in less than a week—but we just get ourselves in more of a bind. We wrap more hair around the matted cocklebur in our paw.

There's relief in surrender. If we would just simply roll over and let God handle it, He will gently unwind and untangle and free us. He removes the burden and the stress and the notion that we have to be superior in all we do. He allows us to be vulnerable and to realize we are nothing without Him. It doesn't matter if we can papier-mâché a life-sized dinosaur or make a killer meatloaf. That means nothing. That's not our identity. That's not truly who we are.

We are daughters (and sons) of the King. We are perfect only in Him. And He sees right through whatever masks we put up.

We will fail. We're expected to stumble. We're even allowed to put a store-bought German chocolate cake in a Tupperware container and try to pass it off as homemade because He loves us anyway.

**THINGS THAT WORK
MY NERVES #42**

Food orders for twenty at the fast-food counter

If you're buying Subway for the entire office, come prepared with a detailed list. No one wants to wait in line while you try to remember if Bobby likes pickles.

Chapter Ten

The J Word

People love to throw the J word around. More often than not, it's an umbrella term used when someone has an opinion, embraces Spirit-led discernment, and holds others accountable. Having an opinion doesn't mean you are judgmental, just like having a tattoo doesn't mean you're a Hells Angel. Embracing Spirit-led discernment doesn't mean you're judgmental—it means you're obedient. Holding others accountable doesn't mean you're passing judgment—it means you're showing love.

You and I make judgments every day. We judge by the weather forecast if we should wear a coat. We judge at what speed we should accelerate our vehicles. We judge whether or not we should purchase a fish plate from the gas station (don't). Exercising judgment is actually a wonderful

> **Embracing Spirit-led discernment doesn't mean you're judgmental— it means you're obedient. Holding others accountable doesn't mean you're passing judgment—it means you're showing love.**

thing. Without it we could end up freezing in a blizzard with diarrhea from the crappie we purchased for $1.99 with our fill-up.

And whether we like it or not, the Holy Bible, our manual for living, has a lot of things to say about judgment. We are told that "bad company corrupts good morals" (1 Cor. 15:33 NASB). This means we should use good judgment when picking friends. We are also told not to lose sight of "wisdom and discretion" (Prov. 3:21 NASB). Again, this is all about using good judgment when making decisions. We're even told not to believe every spirit, but to "test the spirits to see whether they are from God, for many false prophets have gone out into the world" (1 John 4:1 ESV). In other words, I'm going to make a judgment on whether or not the Christians I follow on social media are preaching the real, true Word before I hang on every word they say.

In spite of all this biblical urging, however, some people focus on solely one of many verses in the Bible that refers to judgment: "Judge not" (Matt. 7:1 NKJV). They may not know another single verse in God's Word, but they recite that one at the least hint of criticism or in response to any opinion. They use it as a license to do whatever they want, and no one else can say squat about it.

I am not arguing with what the Bible says when it clearly states that God is our ultimate judge. He will judge my sins. And yours. I can't cast a stone because I am pretty despicable. I've got logs and specks the size of redwoods in my eyes. I admit it. Therefore who am I to judge another's sin? For example, I cannot sit around and gossip that so-and-so drank too much last night. Even after I was saved, but before I came to know Jesus on a more personal level, I could outdrink any *Jersey Shore* cast member.

And that—*that*—is what the Lord is referring to when He tells us to "judge not." We have to recognize we are sinners, no better than any other sinner. We are weak without Him. We are nothing without Him. We need Him as much as the next guy. We need His rescue. We are in debt to what He did for us on the cross. Therefore

I can't judge you, my sister. We are stuck here in this fallen world together. I'm no better than you.

There's a low-budget motel outside of town. It's a junky place—one level, built in the seventies, with only twenty or so rooms. The same cars are always parked there, which leads me to believe people aren't staying there for one or two nights. They're living there long-term.

There's a man who hangs around the parking lot of that motel. He's deathly thin, with sunken cheekbones and dirty, worn clothes. He sits on the tailgate of a rusted, beat-up Nissan truck and watches the traffic. His face appears to be bruised or scabbed, and a cigarette always dangles from his mouth.

I assume this man is addicted to drugs or alcohol. Because of his skinny frame and the bumps on his face, my guess is methamphetamine. Meth addiction is a problem around my town, as it probably is around yours. It's a horrific drug that can take over a person's life very quickly. Meth addicts appear frequently on our local news not only for buying or selling the drug, but also for assault on children and spouses. A few counties over, several meth addicts were recently charged with the murder of a college-aged girl. Evil. The drug is absolutely evil.

Now, I would never pull into that rundown motel, roll down the window, and ask that man to watch my children for a few hours while I run down to Hobby Lobby for some wrought-iron wall décor. I wouldn't leave my children with any stranger as a matter of fact.

Why?

Because good judgment tells me that a stranger and/or drug addict isn't a reliable babysitter.

"Well, Susannah, instead of judging that poor man, why don't you give him some money or offer to help him in some way?"

First, I didn't say the man shouldn't be helped. I said I wouldn't ask him to babysit.

And second, there's a difference in making a judgment and being judgmental.

I recently received a friend request from a girl who went to high school with me. We weren't friends back then, and it wasn't because I was stuck-up or thought I was too good for her. It was because she associated with a group of kids who had been in trouble more than once for doing illegal drugs. I said hello to them in the hallways, but I made a sound judgment call and didn't hop in the back of their Chevrolet Beretta after school for a cocaine run.

I accepted her friend request, and after scrolling through her news feed for only a few seconds, I realized she hasn't changed much since 1998. All of her status updates were hard-core. You know what I mean. She posted about her boyfriend's innocence although he'd been found guilty in a court of law and was doing fifteen years on the inside. She cussed and ranted and raved and incessantly gave the impression through memes and her own thoughts that she didn't "need nobody." She "ain't got time for hoes." Haters were gonna hate. She didn't care what anyone thought of her.

In that activity log cesspool, she wanted to make sure everyone who read her posts understood how tough and independent she was and that only God—although she didn't appear to have any relationship with Him—could judge her. She never mentioned Jesus or His love or His forgiveness. She just twisted that scripture as if to say, "I can act any way I want and I dare you to say anything about it because you aren't God." (If she really took God's judgment seriously, maybe she wouldn't post such vulgar things on the internet.)

Like her, so many think we are judging them simply by disagreeing with them, and we split hairs and become offended when people hold us accountable. When a brother stumbles, Galatians 6:1–2 says, "Brothers, if anyone is caught in any transgression, you who are spiritual should restore him in a spirit of gentleness. Keep watch on yourself, lest you too be tempted. Bear one another's burdens, and so fulfill the law of Christ" (ESV). We all need accountability. I need a sister in Christ to call me out on mistakes. I need Jason to help keep me on the right path. And yet, accountability has become offensive to so many. Is caring that someone is on the wrong path being judgmental?

Is the pope Baptist?

No.

I'm no better than the meth addict loitering in the motel parking lot. I'm no better than the prostitute I saw on *Cops* who said, "I haven't been arrested for prostitution in a long time" and, when the police officer asked, "How long is a long time?" answered, "Three weeks." I'm no better than those kids I knew in high school who had a horrible reputation and were always in trouble. Lord knows I made plenty of mistakes in my high school and college years. I spent so much time in detention for my pranks that I had an assigned seat. I spent a night in jail for drinking and driving. I was a hot mess.

And that girl who friended me on Facebook recently—I'm no better than she is either. But here's the difference: I've realized I can't do life on my own. I've realized being "hard-core" isn't hard-core at all. I realized I'll never be perfect and I need Jesus. And now I have a different kind of wisdom—a wisdom that is associated with the Holy Spirit, who helps me exercise better judgment.

If my mother wasn't dead, I wouldn't dare share this story, because I never told her about it. When I was in my early twenties and a group of friends and I went to see Kid Rock in concert, we rode back to a bar with a group of boys instead of calling a taxi. Gosh, that was stupid. A bunch of vulnerable girls in a truck full of strangers isn't smart—not to mention, one of the boys looked like Skeletor from the *He-Man* shows. (I'm not being judgmental about the guy's appearance. It's a fact. Dead ringer. Skeletor.) Lord knows my mother's prayers for my safety really worked. We could have been raped or murdered or who knows what.

I would never do such a thing today, and I don't think it's just because I'm older and wiser. It's also because of the spirit of discernment I have from God. And that discernment allows me to exercise judgment—yes, *judgment*—in certain situations.

The man in the parking lot—I have prayed for him. When I see him sitting there, my heart goes out to him. He needs Jesus. He is struggling, and I assume his hope is found in drugs instead of the Son. But although I may pray for him and feel for him, I'm still not letting him babysit my children—because I have that discernment.

Having said all that, I do want to address a slightly different form of judgment that has nothing to do with people's immortal souls and not that much to do with the Spirit either. Some judgment is basically opinion—one person's sense of what is decent or acceptable. As you may have noticed, I have a lot of opinions. I feel strongly about them. And I usually have absolutely no problem with expressing them.

I don't wear pajama pants in public. That's not because I think I'm better than those who do, but because when I see someone in Tweety Bird pants at the service desk, I think it looks ridiculous. It's a fashion faux pas similar to the one committed by the lady I saw at Dollar General who was wearing a tube top with bra straps. She had a, um, heavily endowed chest, so her bra straps resembled ratchet straps and were visible to everyone, including astronauts in the space shuttle. She may be saved and spend eternity in the mansion next to mine in heaven, but IMO, no one should wear thick bra straps with a tube top.

A video circulated of me ranting about the dos and don'ts of the school drop-off line. I was deemed judgmental by many commenters because I have an issue with parents carrying on a fifteen-minute conversation about the birds and the bees and giving their kid twelve kisses when they need to kick them out of the car and roll on. (They obviously don't know Carpoolonians 1:3 says, "Thy children shall make haste whilst entering and exiting.")

Again, your mansion may be next to mine, sister, but I sure hope I never get stuck behind you on the streets of gold.

I've learned that if I'm brave enough to express my opinion, I'm going to be called judgmental—not because I'm negative, but because I have a strong point of view. And I'm okay with that. I know I need Jesus just as much as the next sinner, and I know pajama pants are simply not acceptable in public.

THINGS THAT WORK
MY NERVES #62

When people wait two weeks and then reply to my text with "Yeah"

Yeah what? I don't remember what I asked you two weeks ago.
I've deleted my text history. Are you bringing potato salad
to the barbeque? Are you pregnant? Are you going to
be on *Wheel of Fortune*? Are you in danger?
Please clarify.

Chapter Eleven

Let Me Speak to the Manager

I was raised by a no-nonsense mother. Susan didn't take no guff off nobody. She refused to be anyone's doormat. She refused to be taken advantage of. She refused to pay more for a tomato than it was worth.

More times than I can count, I watched my mother while *she* carefully watched the cashier ring up her groceries. She could not be distracted during this critical time. If I dared ask for a pack of gum or money to play the claw machine at the front of the store while her groceries were on the conveyor belt, she quickly snapped her fingers to quiet me. The checkout process was serious business. She knew the price of every single item in that shopping cart, and if she was overcharged by even a penny, she interrupted the entire procedure.

"Dear, those tomatoes are not fifty cents a pound. You rang them up wrong."

If the cashier refused to change the price, my mother would ignore the impatient long line of people behind her and say, "Let me speak to the manager."

There's a certain haircut that, thanks to memes on the internet, has become synonymous with the type of woman who asks for managers. My mother did not have that haircut. She had long, flowing, Farrah Fawcett hair. But Lord have mercy, my mother knew every manager in town. She not only met face-to-face with managers, but she spent a lot of time on the phone with them too. "No, we haven't subscribed to HBO since my daughter watched *Fraggle Rock* fifteen years ago, so I demand that these charges be removed from my bill. If you're unable to do that, then I need to speak with the manager."

As a little girl I lost count of how many times I peered around the heavy purse hanging from my mother's arm and watched her make her complaint to a manager. Mama never cussed anyone out or acted unbecomingly though. She simply and sternly stated her grievance and requested something be done about it. Whether she'd been overcharged or someone working in the store had been rude to her or she was returning something that had played out well before its time, speaking to the manager was her go-to solution.

I didn't mind my mother's brazenness when I was a little kid, but every fifteen-year-old girl is mortified by her mother at times, and I was no exception. When I hit adolescence, I often wished mine would just be quiet and pay the extra dollar for detergent. To avoid the situation, I started grabbing the keys from her purse and bolting out to the car before the word *manager* could escape her lips.

One afternoon I accompanied Mama to Walmart. We pulled into the parking lot, and she asked me to grab a plastic sack from the backseat. She said there was something inside it that needed to be returned to the store. Naturally I peered inside the bag.

"Mama!" I exclaimed. "You cannot return a Conair hair dryer from 1988! Look at the neon font on this thing! And it's in a plastic sack! Do you really think they will give you a refund for this relic? Hair dryers aren't meant to last a lifetime, Mother. Just buy a new one!"

"I was almost *electrocuted* by that thing, Susannah," she said. "It was shooting off sparks and everything. I don't care how old it is; I don't deserve to be killed by it. I deserve reimbursement."

I didn't argue with her. I knew there was no changing her mind. However, I refused to go inside the store. I just knew I would see a friend from school who would overhear my mother complaining to the manager that the ten-year-old hair dryer she'd used while watching *Moonlighting* back in the eighties wasn't up to par. I was sure I'd hear about the event in English class the next day.

I stayed in the car, but you know what? I watched my mother walk out of the store that day with a new and improved hair dryer. I don't know how in the world she convinced the manager to replace a decade-old hair dryer, but she did. And she was reimbursed mighty well.

"This one even has a cold-shot button!" she exclaimed.

Not long after Mama died in 2015, I had the heartbreaking task of going through her things. I laughed out loud, though, when I found a coupon in her kitchen drawer for a free dessert from a local restaurant. The manager of the eatery had included a handwritten note with the coupon: "Dear Ms. Joyner, we are sorry you were not satisfied with the portion size of your Cinna-plosion. Please enjoy one on us next time you visit."

Gosh, I could imagine it so clearly—the waitress bringing the cinnamon-roll dessert to my mama, who then said something like, "Dear, this doesn't look anything like the picture on the menu. This is much smaller than I expected. Let me speak to the manager." After stating her case to a kid in her twenties wearing a button-down shirt, my mother left the restaurant with that coupon and handwritten letter.

I don't want to paint my mother the wrong way, however. Although I used to be embarrassed when she made a complaint and risked ruffling feathers, I understand it better now.

She might've been frugal, but she was not a thief. She didn't spend her whole life trying to rip off grocery stores and superstores and restaurants. And she wasn't a negative old biddy who argued with someone every time she went out in public. She did not complain at every opportunity or enjoy confronting managers.

Mama was simply a widow with very little income who was careful with her money and didn't want to be ripped off. She truly believed she hadn't gotten her money's worth out of that hair dryer or that cinnamon dessert. Susan was going to get her money's worth out of everything she ever purchased. That's the reason she kept the same pink house shoes for a decade. They'd been bleached so many times they were white when she finally threw them away.

Mama was certainly a godly woman. She played piano at our small Baptist church every Sunday and read her Bible daily. She was never ashamed to speak about her relationship with the Lord and His amazing grace. She had a beautiful smile and loved to laugh and make others laugh.

But Mama also had gumption, as Southerners say. She was fun and whimsical, and yet she was adamant in standing up for what she believed in, which meant she had no qualms about publicly disagreeing with someone or something. She didn't waste time talking with the sales associate who had just started working yesterday and didn't have a clue what was going on. She went straight to the top, to the manager.

When something stirs up in my life, I'm often tempted to go to the "associate" first. I hop on the telephone and explain my problem (every mundane detail) to my poor buddy Karen, who can barely get an "mm-hmm" in edgewise.

Karen is a great friend. She loves me. She really does. But she also just wants to get off the dad-gum phone and eat her cheeseburger and watch Netflix, so she usually gives me some quick advice that hasn't been thought through or prayed over, and still I take it as gospel.

Are you guilty of that too? Why don't we get off the phone and go straight to the throne?

God is our Manager—the one in charge, the one running the show, the one everyone reports to. Leave the associate out of it. The Manager is the one who can solve the problem. He's the one who will either answer our prayers the way we ask or not. Either way, He'll do whatever is in our best interest.

If it's His will to reimburse us or reward us, then, mercy, He's going to do it—and He's going to do it big! He's going to give us beauty for ashes and double for our trouble and replace our old, faulty hair dryer for one with a cold-shot button.

Or . . .

He's going to tell us no. He's going to tell us, "That's not what you need." And when He gives us that answer, we can trust that it's the right one. After all, my mother didn't always get what she wanted just because she consulted the manager. She was often told, "Ma'am, I cannot do that." Mama wasn't always pleased with that outcome, but she accepted it—as we need to accept God's no to our complaints and requests.

Recently, as I think back on my mama, her take-it-to-the-top philosophy, and my own relationship to others—including the Lord—I've begun to consider another possibility. Instead of asking for the supervisor only when a problem arises, what if I requested to speak to him or her when I'm really pleased by my experience? In a store or restaurant, for instance, what if I say, "Hey, thanks for running a great place here. I appreciate the good service"? Or "Your bathrooms are so clean, and I appreciate that the soap dispensers are always full"?

I remember one sales associate who probably deserved that extra compliment. It was the day after my beloved godfather, Mr. Charles, died. I'd gone to a department store to find a black dress for the upcoming funeral. Gosh, I was a mess that day. I'd been crying for many hours and hadn't eaten or slept much. I was grieving something terrible. My world seemed so different, so changed, and yet it kept on spinning as if everything was normal for everyone else in that department store. When James Taylor's song "Fire and Rain" came over the speaker while I was in the dressing room, I just sat down and babbled incoherently, especially when I heard the line "I always thought I'd see you one more time again." It was like a tear-jerker scene in a nineties movie.

As I waited in line to purchase the black dress, my phone vibrated with a new e-mail. I looked down and saw that it was Mr. Charles's obituary being sent out by the funeral home. I glanced at my godfather's warm eyes and caring smile in the obituary photo. I thought about the feeling of his mustache against my cheek when he greeted me with a hug. My knees buckled, and everything around me began to spin. Tears fell from my eyes and onto the Ralph Lauren dress I held in my hands.

I'm sure the lady who rang up my purchase saw the sadness in my red, wet, and puffy eyes. Or maybe she didn't, but she was an angel. She complimented the dress. She commented on the lovely autumn weather. She addressed me in a kind, gentle voice. She was patient while my shaking hands searched my wallet for my debit card. There was no way I could have handled a rude employee that day, and rude employees are a dime a dozen, aren't they? That lady's smile, her compassionate eyes with the crinkles in the corners, gave me exactly what I needed at that moment. I wanted to reach across that counter and hug her.

Now I'm thinking, what if I had requested to see the manager just to thank him for hiring this woman—for allowing her to be in my path at that very moment?

And what if I went to God, too, not only with my petitions, but with my praise?

That would be life changing for any of us, wouldn't it? I think we would be more aware of His presence. We would put focus on Him instead of ourselves. We would be reminded of His grace and our redemption. I've found that it's impossible to be in a grumpy, foul, bitter mood while I praise Him. If I'm listening to Christian radio, I cannot help but put my hands up in gratitude. The person at the red light next to my vehicle might think I'm a mime, but who cares? The older I get, the less concerned I am with what people think of me—and the more conscious I am of the amazing grace that surrounds me.

What if I went to God, too, not only with my petitions, but with my praise?

If earthly managers can give us free cinnamon desserts and hair dryers with cold-shot buttons and a just price on a piece of produce, how much more can our heavenly Manager do for us?

Go ahead. Ask for Him. I won't even go hide in the car.

**THINGS THAT WORK
MY NERVES #197**

Rogue facial hair

I just plucked that wiry black hair from my chin a few days ago, and yet it has already returned. When did my youthful peach fuzz turn into a mustache? I glanced in the mirror and thought Si Robertson was wearing my earrings.

Chapter Twelve

Draw the Line

One night when I was seven or eight, I sat on our god-awful burnt-orange corduroy couch and played with my Barbies. My parents sat on the equally as god-awful burnt-orange corduroy loveseat adjacent to me and stared at the Zenith television in the corner of the living room. I'm sure cigarette smoke hovered around the brass ceiling fan in the room and my mother twirled a strand of her long, blonde hair. My daddy probably cradled a Budweiser between the knees of his tattered blue jeans. I don't have a clue what my parents were watching, but I'm sure it was some awesome eighties miniseries or a Neil Young concert.

The heavy rotary phone on the table beside the couch started ringing, and my mother, sitting closest to it, ignored it. She ignored one ring and then two and then three, and then my father finally said, "Susan Ann! Are you going to answer that?"

"No," she said.

Brrrrrrrinnnnnng.

"No?" he asked.

Brrrrrrrinnnnnng.

"No."

Brrrrrrrinnnnnng.

The annoying sound finally ceased, and my father, agitated at Mama's refusal to answer, stated his case. "Susan Ann, when the phone or doorbell rings, a person is meant to answer it."

Mama replied, "Billy Brown, if the phone or doorbell rings and I'm not cooking, eating, reading, or watching a really good movie, then I will answer it."

These were the dreadful days before caller ID and before one could magically pause a television show. Besides, my hypochondriac Aunt Cora was usually the one calling to talk for two hours about her ingrown toenail. Mama considered her time precious, so she would answer the phone and talk to Aunt Cora about her toenail only when she felt like she had the time to do so—and certainly not when *The Thorn Birds* was on.

I absolutely agreed with my mother on this, even at the tender age of eight. I didn't always want to play with the little boy who lived next door. He could be a real butthead and had broken my Pee-wee Herman watch on purpose. My mother was in the shower one Saturday morning when he rang our doorbell, and I didn't even think about leaving my bowl of Smurf-Berry Crunch to answer the door. I was not going to let my cereal get soggy and waste the seconds it took to walk to the front door and tell him to buzz off.

I practiced this nonchalance for years. When I was in my twenties, I had a very demanding friend. She called me *all* day. She often showed up uninvited to my home. She made plans for us without consulting me first. I was once dragged on a surprise outing to a craft show, which was absolute torture because I loathed crafts—so much so that in third grade I'd told my Vacation Bible School teacher to just teach me about the love of Jesus and leave the Popsicle sticks out of it.

My demanding friend meant well, I know. She just wanted us to do things together, but she had no sense of boundaries. To me, what she deemed friendship was nothing more than smothering. But instead of addressing this with her, I did what many of us have done in similar situations. I didn't answer her calls, ignored her texts, and made up lies about why I couldn't go somewhere with her. She eventually just left me alone.

I never had the courage to say, "I don't want to do that today. Thank you though." I feared I would hurt her feelings if I didn't comply with all the things she wanted me to do. And Lord, I hate hurting feelings, although I'm sure ignoring her was the biggest hurt of all.

My eyes were opened, though, when a friend from high school came into town for a weekend and I texted her to ask when we could get together. I found her brutally authentic response refreshing: "I'll be honest. I don't want to do anything when I get home but hang out with my mom and sisters." My feelings were not hurt when I read that reply, yet they would have been if she'd spent the whole weekend coming up with fifteen different excuses as to why we couldn't get together. She had a mission—to spend time with certain people—and she stuck to it. And by being honest and matter-of-fact about her boundaries in this matter, she taught me an important lesson.

Boundaries like that are so vitally necessary, healthy, and helpful. We have to get over the fear of hurting feelings, boldly draw a line, and say, "Hey, you aren't allowed to cross this." We don't have to be aggressive or rude, but we do have to be firm and clear and stick to our guns. And when we do, most people will follow our lead.

What do we do when our boundaries are ignored though? That recently happened when I spoke at a charity event one evening. I stepped off the stage after my talk to mingle with the guests and gorge on fancy finger foods. I had the pleasure of speaking with people who had read my books and wanted to discuss them. One kind lady confided in me about the recent death of her mother, and although I'd never met her, we hugged each other and cried together for about ten minutes. And then she left.

But one woman stayed. She had followed me around the entire evening, yet had never spoken to me. Whenever I attempted to make eye contact, she would look down at the glass of champagne in her hand. She'd even stood in a corner and watched me while the crowd dwindled and the venue staff cleaned plates from the tables and removed props from the stage.

I asked several people who the woman was, and no one knew. So I approached her and asked how she was doing. I was a little anxious—what if she put a box cutter to my throat? But she was very nice and said she followed me on social media and had driven several hours to see me speak. We took a photo together, and I assumed she had avoided talking or making eye contact with me throughout the evening solely because she was shy or I made her nervous, though the latter is absolutely ridiculous because I put my pants on one leg at a time like everyone else—and, since I'm pregnant while writing this, sometimes fall onto the wall while doing so.

After our brief chat and photo, I thought she would leave, but she didn't. Almost all of the guests were gone, but she had decided to stay. My husband wasn't with me that night, but a friend and her husband who happened to see my predicament offered to walk me to my car so I would not end up the subject of a Hallmark Mysteries movie.

Believe it or not, that woman followed us to the parking lot! My heart began to pound in my chest, and I admit I even considered calling the police. I refrained, though, thinking maybe she just really did appreciate my humor and my videos.

On the ride home, though, I became livid. I decided it's not okay to make a person feel the way she made me feel—uncomfortable and threatened. It's not okay to stand in a corner and creepily peer over a champagne glass at someone. It's really not okay to hang around after an event is over and follow a person to the parking lot. I did not appreciate her overstepping my boundaries the entire evening. She'd been nice to me when we spoke, but she'd had no respect for my space.

That kind of harassment is the very purpose of boundaries. The lines you draw are meant to protect you from physical or mental harm. And if your healthy boundaries make someone feel uncomfortable, angry, or bad in some sort of way, that's just fine. It is perfectly acceptable to say, "Back off, sister. You aren't allowed to treat me this way."

Boundaries are God's idea. Followers of Christ are encouraged to stay within certain bounds in this world. We are told not to mingle with people who exhibit sinful behaviors or live the way the lost do (which sometimes means we're called judgmental).

We set rules for children to follow, lines they aren't allowed to cross. Isn't it just as important to set some rules for ourselves too?

Just as we set limits for our children because we love them, we have to love ourselves enough to do the very same. I don't let my children ride their ATVs without helmets or jump off the pontoon boat without a life preserver. They aren't allowed to watch R-rated movies or knock on the neighbor's door at seven o'clock on a Saturday morning (mamas, please teach your children this lifesaving boundary too).

We set rules for children to follow, lines they aren't allowed to cross. Isn't it just as important to set some rules for ourselves too?

If you have a hard time doing this—or if respecting other people's boundaries is a challenge for you—ask the Lord to help. After all, boundaries bear a direct correlation to self-control, which the Bible calls a fruit of the Spirit (Galatians 5). Pray, "Jesus, help me control my actions and not text anyone twenty-three times an hour or follow anyone to a parking lot." And "Lord, give me the strength to tell anyone who crosses the line to step back."

Then take a deep breath and . . . do it. My mama would be so proud of you!

**THINGS THAT WORK
MY NERVES #12**

Deafening decibels in a department store

Because of the obscenely loud music, I can barely
concentrate enough to read the price tags.
I'm here for a romper, not a rave.

Chapter Thirteen

What in the World?

✦

Teen Beat.

The Coreys (Feldman and Haim), Kirk Cameron, and Debbie Gibson all looked back at me from the cover of the magazine while I stood in the grocery store line with my mother. I was young and impressionable, and the temptation was overwhelming. I had to know Feldman's favorite dessert, Kirk's quirks, and Debbie's makeup tips. I threw a copy on top of Mama's groceries, and she agreed that I could get it—as long as the cashier rang it up correctly.

That's where my obsession with pop culture began, and it grew with every *Teen Beat, YM, Teen People,* and *Seventeen* I read. By the age of fifteen, I had a wealth of knowledge. I knew album names and song titles from my parents' classic rock to UB40 and everything in between. I knew the birthdays, likes, and dislikes of my favorite celebrities. The eight-by-twelve wall in my bedroom was a shrine to Leonardo DiCaprio. I craved gossip about Nick Lachey and Jessica Simpson and needed to know what color blush Jennifer Love Hewitt suggested for my skin tone. What did TLC wear to the Grammys? I knew music, movies, slang, hot items, popular lipstick colors, concert dates, guest appearances on television shows, live interviews, famous breakups, marriages, divorces. I knew the world—or at least the world of pop culture.

Not only did I know it, I followed it too. I was all up in it. I caved to peer pressure and snuck out of the house to smoke cigarettes and drink wine coolers. I rented movies chock-full of awful language and repeated what I heard. I didn't care if the popular kids were rude and cruel to other kids; I wanted to be a part of their group solely because they were popular. I don't like to admit it, but I mistreated many people on my mission to reach "the top." The world—living for it and living in it—was my idol.

My vast wealth of pop-culture knowledge began to fade when I married at twenty-four and had my first child at twenty-five. After that I spent the days watching the Disney Channel and Nickelodeon instead of MTV and TMZ. I listened to Baby Einstein CDs in the car. I knew more about the terrible twos than Top 40. I realized I'd become seriously out of touch when I played trivia at the local sports bar one night and didn't even place in the top ten.

Now strangers grace the covers of the magazines at the grocery store. Jimmy Fallon interviews celebrities born in the late nineties that I've never heard of. I haven't watched a music award show since Brandy and Monica argued over who the boy belonged to. I'm disoriented when my daughter plays her Spotify playlist or shows me videos of YouTube celebrities or says something like, "Ashlyn just spilled the tea!" I am confused by the lyrics, wonder how such stupidity went viral, and assume Ashlyn needs a towel.

Then I think, *I've turned into my mother.*

When I was a teen, my mama couldn't care less about pop culture either. She shook her head at my Leonardo shrine and said he couldn't hold a candle to James Dean or Paul Newman. She hadn't been to a concert since ZZ Top came to Memphis in 1985, and she was perfectly content with that. Mama thought all the new bands were garbage. When I asked for one-hundred-twenty-dollar tickets to see Smashing Pumpkins, she looked at me quizzically and said I could destroy gourds at home for free.

There's nothing wrong with knowing the hottest bands and television shows, but it's no longer something I'm interested in, and it's certainly not my idol. I believe both maturing as an adult and growing spiritually are the reasons for my nonchalance when it comes to things of the world. I'm not a young and impressionable teen anymore, and I believe our culture has taken a negative turn over the last several decades. More than ever before, our world now relishes in calling evil good and good evil, and I want no part of it.

I was reminded of this one December evening when my husband, kids, dogs, and I were all cozy on the couch with hot chocolate and sugar cookies, watching Christmas movies on a popular network station. When the commercial break came on, we were suddenly transported from the North Pole to the backseat of a convertible, where underage kids were doing things that would be more appropriate for the movies shown on Cinemax on a Saturday night in the

> **I believe both maturing as an adult and growing spiritually are the reasons for my nonchalance when it comes to things of the world.**

nineties. Because I couldn't find the remote beneath the mounds of blankets and pillows, I reached over to shield my children's innocent eyes and loudly sang "Bohemian Rhapsody" to cover the sounds of teens moaning and slobbering as they removed clothing. (I don't know why I chose "Bohemian Rhapsody." It was just the first thing to pop into my mind.)

I may be out of touch, but no seven- or eleven-year-old needs to see high school kids having sex in a car. I didn't even want to see it. What genius thought that commercial would be appropriate to broadcast right after Frosty received a corncob pipe and a button nose?

That's the world we live in though. Sex is glorified above all. "If it feels good, do it" is shouted from the rooftops. People are sleeping around, young girls dress like exotic dancers, no one can stay committed to one person anymore, and anyone with a moral stance who dares to address today's standards is called a prude or old-fashioned or judgmental. There's so much in this world that is sin, and yet the world calls it "fun."

I think of what the Bible says in James 4:4: "Don't you know that friendship with the world means enmity against God? Therefore, anyone who chooses to be a friend of the world becomes an enemy of God." And Romans 12:2 also addresses this by saying, "Do not conform to the pattern of this world, but be transformed by the renewing of your mind. Then you will be able to test and approve what God's will is—his good, pleasing and perfect will."

I was conformed to this world when I was in high school and college, but today I am often convicted when I participate in something worldly that I know I shouldn't. Just recently I was watching a popular movie and felt incredibly uneasy in my spirit. The world gave the movie five stars, but I knew the Holy Spirit was nudging me to turn it off. I recently heard a song that I loved in high school on the radio, but the lyrics were so raunchy that I had to change the station and put on some Hillsong worship music to redeem myself.

As the children's song says, we have to be careful what our little eyes see and what our little ears hear. When I hung around with certain people as a kid, my mother could tell. She used to say, "You have such a bad attitude! You must have been hanging around with _____!" (I'm not mentioning the name in case _____ reads this book.) I am thirty-seven years old, but that still happens. The world still has an influence on me. When I'm around gossipers, I tend to gossip. When I'm around cursers, I might find myself cursing.

But when I leave the presence of the gossipers and the cursers (or whatever), I feel a conviction for what I've done or said.

I know the gossiping and the cursing wasn't the Lord within me. That was the world. That was the world influencing me. But it's not what I want. Not anymore. I want more than this world and its music and movies and sports teams and award shows. I want intangible things—the glory and joy that can only be found in heaven. I want to see my mother and father and grandparents again.

That's why I don't focus solely on the here and now or what song hit the number-one spot for the twelfth week in a row. This world isn't the be-all and end-all for me. I want what comes after. I want the prize that is offered after running this race known as life.

But I'm not a hermit. I don't live in a hut in the middle of the woods and forage on berries and keep warm with a solar-powered furnace. I do live here—in a specific town and a particular region of the country and with a particular culture all around me. And I do still enjoy music and movies and a good novel. But I don't worship these things. I don't want to be so consumed by popular culture and what is trending that I lose sight of what is eternal. I don't want to be Demas.

Demas was a friend of Paul and a follower of Christ. He was with Paul during his second imprisonment in Rome, and Paul considered him a faithful friend. However, Demas soon abandoned Paul and the call to spread the Word of God. Second Timothy 4:10 tells us why Demas left—because he loved the world. That's right. He succumbed to the temptation to join the hip and happening culture of Thessalonica.

Demas chose the temporary benefits of the world instead of the eternal riches found in Christ. And once Demas abandoned Paul, he wasn't heard from again. One can assume, however, that his commitment to the world was not beneficial. It never is.

First John 2:15 tells us not to love the world or the things of the world and says that, if we do, the love of the Father is not within us. This is because we cannot serve two masters. We cannot love the Lord and all that He stands for and love the world at the same time. In fact, that would be an oxymoron, wouldn't it?

When I was in church youth group, a girl sat on the pew in front of me one Wednesday night, and her shirt read,

> This world is not my home
> though it seems to be.
> My world is in a place
> God has prepared for me.

I sometimes thought of that little rhyme when I studied *YM* like it was the Bible. And then I'd shrug it off because heaven was a far-off place and a long time away, and Jared Leto was going to tell me sixteen things guys wanted *right now*.

What in the world was I thinking?

THINGS THAT WORK
MY NERVES #7

Murphy's Law

If I run to the store with messy hair, zero makeup, a stained T-shirt, and shorts I've owned since Bush One was in office, I'm bound to see everyone I know.

Chapter Fourteen

Faith over Fame

Okay, sisters, are y'all ready? This chapter is going to ruffle feathers. You'll probably squint your eyes, purse your lips, and be tempted to throw this book across the room. Or it's possible that this chapter may open your eyes. That's what I pray will happen, because I'm more concerned with eyes than feathers.

If you look at your social media news feed right now—don't actually do it; you'll fall down a rabbit hole—maybe you'll discover the girl who sat next to you in tenth-grade algebra is gluten-free. You'll realize some cats are scared of cucumbers. You'll watch a video of someone lip-syncing in the car. Then you'll fall down another rabbit hole. And another. And you'll forget to finish reading my book.

Anyway, I guarantee there is a Christian woman posting in your news feed right now. She's probably a wife and a mother. She regularly posts status updates to remind you that it's okay not to have it all together. She puts a Sierra filter on a photo of her laundry and maybe humorously captions it, "I can do all things through Christ . . ." Maybe she has millions of followers or maybe only a dozen—either

117

way, a visit to her page reassures you that motherhood is messy, marriage is messy, life is messy. She makes you feel better about the path you're on. She reminds you it's both okay to cry and okay to be happy.

Maybe this woman is me. If so—*takes a bow*—thank you.

The Lord uses social media. He doesn't need it, but He certainly has many vessels posting updates that point people to Him on the daily. However, those Grandmaw Lucy referred to as "wolves in sheep's clothing" have Facebook and Twitter accounts too.

They're not easy to recognize, of course, because they preach what is popular and voice their opinions as gospel. They teach a "self-help" theology and subtly worship themselves, their strengths, and even their weaknesses, and they encourage other women to do the same. Essentially they rely on themselves and not on God, and they aren't teaching humility or the truth found in the Bible.

> **The Lord uses social media. He doesn't need it, but He certainly has many vessels posting updates that point people to Him on the daily.**

Second Timothy 4:3–4 says, "For there is going to come a time when people won't listen to the truth but will go around looking for teachers who will tell them just what they want to hear. They won't listen to what the Bible says but will blithely follow their own misguided ideas" (TLB).

I believe that time is now.

A few popular ideas about Jesus on social media especially grieve my heart—and I think they must grieve the heart of God too.

Jesus Is Like Jerry Garcia

There's this notion that Jesus is a free-loving hippie with sunglasses and a beard floating around in a VW van with arms outstretched, full of acceptance for all. He says things like, "Hey, man, just be who you want to be. As long as you are kind to others, everything else is cool. Do what feels good and what makes you happy."

Now, I like Jerry Garcia as much as the next Deadhead, and *Box of Rain* is a classic, but he's not Jesus. Jerry Garcia isn't my teacher or mentor, and he sure didn't die on a cross for my sins. My Lord doesn't float around in a pastel van giving groovy motivational speeches. Instead He says profound things like, "Deny yourself and follow Me."

There was a time when I loved drinking. More precisely, I loved getting drunk. I loved knowing there was a cooler full of beer and a karaoke machine within reach. I've told some of my funniest jokes and laughed the hardest and had the most fun when I was three sheets to the wind. And although I don't live that lifestyle anymore, my flesh still craves it from time to time. My flesh still craves partying with my friends, even though my flesh also knows that nothing but trouble comes from it—trouble in the form of waking up the next day with a pounding headache, cotton mouth, nausea, and terrible regret over something I said or did.

But denying ourselves means knowing that even though something is fun and our flesh gravitates toward it, it's off-limits if God says no. We are to live according to His Word and His purpose, not our own desires.

That's the complete opposite of what Jerry Garcia Jesus says.

Jesus Is Like Ron Swanson from *Parks and Rec*

Another popular idea is the absurd teaching that God is like Ron Swanson—the director of the Parks and Recreation Department in fictional Pawnee, Indiana. Ron is the man in charge, but he gives an incredible amount of leeway to his staff and doesn't implement rules or consequences. People really think God doesn't care what we do and just nonchalantly watches our lives the way we watch our screens. *Facepalm.*

How can any person who claims to be a Christian not know there are countless scriptures in the Bible that say the very opposite? I cannot judge your sin because I'm as much of a sinner as you, but our God is blameless and is the only judge. He decides the consequences for our sin. Just as Granny Rebecca made me get a switch from her tree and tore up my backside after I obeyed my flesh, colored with her new Avon eye palette, and then lied about it, the Lord, our judge, punishes us for our sin. He doesn't light up our backside with a hickory switch, but out of love and concern for us, He most certainly teaches us a lesson when we act a fool.

Envisioning Jesus as being a guy with no consequences also allows us to believe that everyone is going to heaven as long as they are "nice." I'm not a heavyset preacher screaming about hell and damnation behind a pulpit while my face turns beet red and beads of sweat the size of butterbeans fall from my temples, but I do know the only way to heaven is through salvation—confessing our sins and asking Jesus into our hearts, relying solely upon Him to save us—not through our own good works. Sorry to be the bearer of bad news, but baking cookies, washing cars, and selling raffle tickets won't get you into heaven by themselves.

Does that make you mad? Well, here's something to make your blood pressure skyrocket: hell is full of nice people. If you're offended by that, you should get out your Bible and read John 14: 6, where Jesus says He is the only way. Sorry, it's not my policy. It's the Manager's.

Of course, our Savior is the definition of love and tells us to come to Him just as we are, but He never tells us to stay where we are. Instead, He says He's going to make us a new creation. He promises to change us. If we aren't open to changing, then we aren't true followers of Christ.

Jesus Is Like Oprah

All over social media there's a trend that the women just eat up. It goes something like this:

> Girl, you can do anything you want and be anyone you want to be. You have the power. Your entire destiny is up to you. You decide the trajectory of your life. You don't need anyone to make your dreams come true—all you need is inside of you. You are woman—roar!

That. That right there is foolish. It sounds good. It makes you want to jump up from your couch and put on your tennis shoes and take a twelve-mile jog while Aretha Franklin blasts from your earbuds. I know. It made me want to do the same thing while I was typing it. But it's folly. Allow me to reword it with some truth:

> Girl, you can do all things through Christ who gives you strength. You are weak, but He is strong. The Lord has a good, good plan for your life—a plan for a hope and a future. He is the author of your desires and knows what is best for you. All you need is Him. You are a daughter of the king—roar.

You see that? I took the emphasis off of you and put it on Him. That's truth. And it still makes me want to listen to Aretha.

When I wasn't following Jesus, back when I was enjoying Miller Lite and Mötley Crüe on karaoke nights, I didn't want to change. I loved those things, and even though I thought I loved Jesus, I was living for the weekend. I also didn't want to stop because stopping would be painful. I didn't want to give up the nightlife. It wasn't until I meditated on the scriptures that clearly state drunkenness is sin (such as Eph. 5:18, Gal. 5:21, and 1 Cor. 11:21) that I finally took up my cross and followed Him instead of entering another dance contest at Coyote Ugly.

If you aren't growing and changing, you are not where you need to be in your relationship with Christ. If, instead, you are believing as gospel what some woman on the internet said when she posted, "I love Jesus, but I do this" and "I love Jesus, but I do that"—and "this" and "that" are clearly defined as sin in the Bible—then you don't truly want to follow Him. And you liking her status sends the message that you're agreeing with a mere mortal instead of the Word of God.

Although He truly loves her, and you and me, and asks us to follow Him, Jesus also says, "Go and sin no more" (John 8:11 TLB). He died on the cross for our sins, and if what wolves preach is true—that we can do whatever we want, sin however we want, be whoever we want, and Jesus will approve—then what was the point of Him dying on the cross? What was the point of Him bleeding and suffering if sin isn't a real thing?

I wish there was a scripture that said, "As long as you go to church on Sunday and tithe and smile at strangers and hold doors open for elderly ladies, you can do whatever else you want." But there ain't.

Women, especially women who are at the end of their rope, with messy kitchens and screaming toddlers and husbands working late hours, are duped more than anyone else. They are in need of a spiritual connection—a virtual friend—and they are too exhausted to dig into God's Word, so they take as gospel what these also exhausted and messy Christian internet stars say. It is my fervent prayer that I never let anything come from my mouth or my fingertips that does not align 100 percent with the infallible Word of God. I never want to teach what's popular instead of what's true.

Don't believe any of this because I say it. Or because Beth Moore says it. (Hey, Beth! Call me! Love you!) Don't believe it because your mama or grandmother said it.

Believe it because the Word says it.

Believe it because the Word is true.

**THINGS THAT WORK
MY NERVES #93**

When someone says,
"You clean up nicely"

I think they're really saying, "You usually look quite average
or even borderline ugly, so it's refreshing to see you in
something other than yoga pants and a stained sweatshirt.
I'm also pleased that your face has been covered
with foundation, although a paper bag
would have worked as well."

Chapter Fifteen

Surrender Takes Time

On a cold December evening, as I sat on my couch and worked on this very book, my sweet Malshipoo, Pepper, pawed at my hand to let me know she needed to go potty. I was at a stopping point anyway, so I put my computer to the side, scooped up her sleeping brother, Nutella (a.k.a. Newt), and walked to the door. They both yawned from their winter nap and walked onto the front porch while my heavy, pregnant body welcomed the cold night air.

They were standing only ten feet from the door—ten feet from me—when Pepper began to bark. I assumed a deer must've been somewhere in the darkness of our front yard, but before I could call them inside, Newt disappeared into the night—barking as ferociously as a Maltese / shih tzu / poodle mix can. And then the barking was replaced with pitiful cries.

Pepper rushed back into the house as I tore down the hallway to wake Jason, who had been asleep in our bed for hours. I was borderline hysterical, and both Natalie and Bennett rushed downstairs to see what was wrong. When they saw me screeching and crying, they both began to cry too.

"Something happened to Newt, Jason! A coyote got Newt!"

"No! Not my Newt!" Bennett screamed at the top of his lungs and ran onto the porch to look for his buddy.

We hear coyotes many nights deep in the woods behind the house. They eerily howl back and forth, and my biggest fear from the moment we purchased this land was that one might come into the yard and attack Newt or Pepper. (My children are too big to interest a hungry coyote.)

So soon after we built our home and moved in, I taped a picture of Newt, Pepper, and our Boykin spaniel, Tucker, to the wall in my prayer closet, and beneath it I posted scriptures about protection. I also wrote, "God, please encamp angels around my animals and protect them from coyotes, snakes, heartworms, and anything that would cause them harm. Give them long lives, Jesus." Maybe it sounds absurd, but I even placed hands on my dogs and prayed for their safety.

My fears about coyotes subsided after that because I had faith God would do what I'd requested in ink and in spoken prayer. Every night, when I let my beloved dogs out to potty, I had faith that those words wouldn't return void. I had faith there were angels over Newt, Pepper, Tucker, and our newest dog, a German shepherd mix named Ella, everywhere they went on this property. I wasn't worrying about the coyotes howling in the woods behind the house because Jesus was protecting my animals.

But that night, as Jason threw on clothes, grabbed his flashlight, and ran out the front door to look for Newt, I knew a coyote had gotten him. When a pack of them began to howl not far from our front yard, I knew my buddy was gone, and I was overcome with physical sickness.

Some people don't know the bond between a dog and a person,

and that's okay. If you're one of those people, you probably think I'm nuts to allow the death of a dog to shake me to my core. For me, however, my dogs are more than just dogs. I believe my pets are truly a gift from God and put on this earth just for me. I refuse to call them "fur babies," but they are certainly integral to our family.

Nutella had been my Kleenex when Mama died. He'd followed every step I took and slept on my pillow every night. He'd cuddled up next to me for every blog post and book I wrote. While I was going through a long season of infertility, he'd been like a baby who loved to be swaddled and held close. He'd filled a void in my life.

No, Nutella wasn't just some dog. He was my companion, my sidekick, and my best friend until the day he died.

My sweet husband tirelessly walked our property and looked for Newt. He finally found him early the next morning and brought his lifeless body back to the house. Thankfully the coyote had quickly killed him and then dropped him, so he wasn't bloody or disfigured. Still, we were devastated. Hours before, when I'd picked him up from the couch where he'd been sleeping cozily by my side, I had taken note of how warm he was. I'd even commented on it as I carried him to the porch door—carried him to his death. And now he was cold and without a breath in his fuzzy body.

We buried him in a beautiful wooded area in the backyard the next day. I sat on a pile of muddy leaves in pajama pants and a sweatshirt and cried over that dog nearly as much as I had cried over my mother's grave three years ago. I didn't just cry because I was heartbroken at the loss. I also cried because I was angry. I was angry at myself, for letting him outside. And I was angry with God.

A few days after Newt died, I stood in the drizzling rain, six months pregnant, wearing an ill-fitting raincoat and Jason's mud boots because my feet were too swollen to wear my own. Some trash had blown into our yard, so I slowly bent over to pick up each piece. When I reached the section of grass where Newt had been killed,

I looked up to the gray, wintry sky and began yelling at the Lord. I threw my hands up while tears soaked my cheeks and screamed as loudly as I could, "Why did You let this happen? I thought You heard my prayers! I can't trust You anymore!"

I'll admit it was dramatic, but it was also real, and it was raw. I had never been that angry and yelled at God like that—not even when my parents died or when I miscarried. I'd always been too afraid to do such a thing. Who was I to yell at the Maker of the universe? In the past I had feared He would smite me with a flash of lightning for such a thing. But on that cold, rainy December day, pregnant and hormonal and missing my dog terribly, I couldn't contain my anger.

I believed I'd done so much for the Lord in the months before Newt died. I had written my book *Can't Make This Stuff Up!* for Him. I'd always been scared to death of public speaking, but I'd ventured out of my comfort zone to speak to churches about His love and mercy and forgiveness. I shared my testimony of hope and restoration. I praised Him publicly for carrying me through the deaths of my parents and miscarriage and infertility. When I got pregnant with our third child after six years of trying, I told the whole internet that He still performs miracles and that faith and prayer really work. I spent hours answering e-mails and pointing the lost and the hurt toward Him.

And yet God had allowed my dog to die so suddenly and tragically. Hadn't I been through enough loss in my life? I found so much comfort and joy in Newt, so why would God let him be killed in a way that I so feared? What was the point? What was the lesson? Why pray and write in a prayer closet if God was just going to do whatever He wanted anyway?

But that's not even how God works. He doesn't say, "If you do something good for me, I'll do something good for you." That's a human principle, not a godly one.

Some might argue, "Well, Susannah, you're reading too much into it. It was just a dog. He got killed by a coyote. God didn't have a thing to do with it. He wasn't punishing you. It's just one of those things."

But I sure didn't see it that way at the time. The death of Nutella completely rocked my faith.

More times than I can count, I had thanked God for the acres of wooded land where we live. Before the house was even built, I'd walked the property and prayed blessings over it. I'd walked across the very yard where Newt was killed and requested that angels be placed there. I'd walked along the pasture and thanked Him for the land where my children would play and my dogs would run and generations to come would make memories.

But when Newt died, this place that had given me such peace and joy suddenly felt scary and foreign. It became a place where predators lurked in the shadows. It's where I had stood helpless on my porch and heard my beloved dog die in the dark.

I was broken and anxious. While I should have been celebrating the impending birth of a new child—a child that was no doubt a miracle and promise from God—I was instead questioning the struggle and the disappointment. I wished our land conjured happiness instead of sorrow. I wished I didn't keep replaying the sights and sounds of Newt's death each time I looked out the window. I wished my faithful friend was still by my side.

As I wished and mourned, old wounds broke open. I hurt a little more each time I saw poor Pepper moping around the house or looking out the window for her brother. I was back in a familiar place of longing and loneliness—a place I hadn't been in since Mama died. A place I hadn't expected to be back in so soon.

In *Can't Make This Stuff Up!* I had written that Jesus is our lawyer during life's trials. He's there in the simple moments and the sorrow. He reveals purpose in pain. And now, although I was grieving and so angry with God, I still believed all that to be true. As I mourned Newt and the peace I used to associate with my front-porch view, I was still confident I needed God. But I refused, in my stubborn anger, to sing praises to Him during church service, and I lost all desire to read His Word. I became hardheaded and hard-hearted, but I knew I would eventually draw close to Him again.

I also knew it would take time.

And it certainly did.

Crazy as it sounds, we aren't always ready to fall into His arms. As believers we know God will grow us in our times of trouble and heartache, but we don't want to hear that. We know Scripture says He "causes all things to work together for good to those who love" Him (Rom. 8:28 NASB), but we still question and doubt. We know that pressure produces strength and the fire produces refinement, but we don't care. We just want to feel the grief. We need to feel it. We need to mourn and question and cry. We need to sit with our sorrow and talk some things out.

That's exactly what I did after Newt died. It took several long months before I could trust and thank the Lord for His plan—even if I still didn't understand it.

It's inevitable that our faith will be tested at times. Sometimes that test is from the enemy. The devil will use anything, even a dog, to keep us from drawing close to Jesus. He will do all he can to convince us God isn't good. He might even have said to God, in some biblical, Job-like way, "Let Susannah miscarry that child in her womb. She'll quit praising You then." And God might have answered, "I won't take that baby, but I'll take that beloved dog of hers. She'll praise me anyway." Or maybe Newt was going to be jealous of my new baby and snap at her. Or maybe I made my adored dog an idol for too long.

I kept thinking there has to be some reason why—some per-spective I'll never understand this side of heaven—the Lord, in

His infinite wisdom, allowed Newt to die. I recognize I may sound absurd and may have overanalyzed this whole thing, but I still wanted so badly to make sense of the heartache. I still wanted my earthly mind to comprehend it all.

You'd think I would have learned by now that sometimes we just won't understand. The Bible even tells us not to lean on our own understanding. I'll never perceive why Daddy died of a heart attack while I was home alone with him or why my mother died the day after we had a petty argument or why I miscarried, but as I discuss in *Can't Make This Stuff Up!*, whatever trial we go through, no matter how painful or debilitating, can be considered a gift if it points us to Jesus.

> He'll still be there, unmoved, when we are ready to let go of the rope and fall into His arms. He always holds on to us, even when we're not holding on to Him.

Until we surrender and return to the Lord's arms, we may be angry—and surrender may take time. We may swear off K-LOVE and church and Bible study and our own testimony of how good God has been to us in the past. I've learned that's okay. He can handle it. He can handle our anger. And how we feel doesn't change who He is. He'll still be there, unmoved, when we are ready to let go of the rope and fall into His arms.

He always holds on to us, even when we're not holding on to Him.

Men with "I love my wife" bumper stickers on their vehicles

These cause arguments between wives and their husbands who don't have "I love my wife" bumper stickers.

Chapter Sixteen

Stop Believing the Lies

As I write these words, I am now nine months pregnant with our Annabeth. She's due any day now, and every time she violently kicks my bladder, I think of all the prayers sent up for her. After six years of waiting and countless infertility medications and methods, she was conceived naturally a few weeks after my thirty-seventh birthday.

During the Annabeth waiting period, Satan lied to me quite a bit. Although I believed my desire for a third child to be God-given, the devil told me it just wasn't going to happen. When we built our home, he told me I was a fool to designate a room as the nursery and write scripture about God's promises and Sarah's conception on the studs. He told me I was an idiot to keep praying for the same thing each and every day. Some days I believed him and pouted and cried and got all in my feelings (Natalie cringes when I say that) and ate Little Debbie cakes by the dozen. Other days I told him to shut the hell up, walked straight to the baby department at Target, and bought a onesie.

People tend to get offended at the mention of Satan. I have talked about "the enemy" before and had people look at me like I was a turd in a punch bowl. They don't want to believe there is a real adversary roaming around and seeking to kill, steal, and destroy—an angel named Lucifer who turned proud, cocky, and greedy and was thrown out of heaven, as described in Ezekiel 28:14–17. Sounds a lot like something Stephen King or Bram Stoker would come up with, doesn't it? But Satan is as real as the mouse I hear chewing on insulation in my attic right now.

If you have given your heart to Jesus, Satan hates you. He doesn't just roll his eyes when he sees you coming. He doesn't just dart into the ballpark bathroom to avoid conversation with you. He wants nothing more than to shut you up, ruin your life, place you in bondage, break your heart, and prohibit you from being the hands and feet of Jesus. He desires to wage war against you. He hates you more than Michael Scott hates Toby Flenderson.

Satan studies us for a while, and when he's come up with a plan to tear us apart, he starts with our minds. He's no idiot. He knows our thoughts usually manifest themselves as our speech and actions. He will plant a terrible idea or a seed of doubt in that head of ours, and we will usually do the rest. We dwell on those seeds and believe them, and suddenly we are speaking curses over our own lives and situations and end up in a downward spiral of self-loathing, pity, and downright depression.

I firmly believe this is the way suicidal thoughts begin. What would please the devil more than a dearly loved and cherished child of God ending his or her life early and robbing this world of the gifts and blessings God intended to be shared with others?

Once Satan plants a lie in the mind, he plants another one. That lie says, "Satan isn't real." That's mind-blowing, isn't it? Satan never wants to take credit for his work. Instead, he wants you to think the thoughts in your mind are your own.

For instance, have you ever thought something horrible about another person or situation? And then you thought, *Mercy! What a despicable person I am to think such a thing!* You continued to dwell on it and felt guilty and dirty and ashamed for even thinking it in the first place. That thought probably wasn't even yours to begin with, my friend. It was planted there by fallen angel Lucifer. Your thought life becomes his garbage dump. And that garbage includes all the yucky things, including doubt and insecurity and hate and shame and fear.

Most often, Satan starts with questions: "Why?" Or "If God really loved you, wouldn't He . . . ?" If we allow those two questions to take over our minds, they can mess up a sister real quick.

And what about these doozies?

"You'd be happier with her husband." Girl, no.

"You're an awful mother." Nope.

"You can't do anything right." Again with Satan's craziness.

"Even Jesus can't forgive you of that." Invalid.

"What's the point?" Shut your mouth.

"You should do something different with your hair." Don't fall for it, ladies. Stick to the color/cut combo you know.

Unless we rebuke these lies and recognize they are an attempt to defeat us, they have the potential to ruin our lives. You may find yourself in an affair with your best friend's husband *and* sporting a mullet and brassy highlights.

It's easy to fall under a spell of spiritual attack. Ephesians 6:12 tells us we don't wrestle flesh and blood. We wrestle forces we cannot see. It's not Stephen King fiction. It's real. And a lot of the battle happens inside our heads.

Back when I was in college, I worked full-time at a church day care while going to class at night. A woman named Jacqueline (not her real name—I just heard it on television and thought it would be a good one to use) worked in the toddler room next to my room. I smoked at the time and so did Jacqueline, so we took breaks together.

During our conversations over the ashtray in the maintenance shop behind the church, Jacqueline (I should've picked a shorter name) never had anything positive to say. She'd inhale the smoke and then declare, "These things are going to kill me." Then she'd speak negatively about her marriage, declaring, "He'll never be faithful to me." She'd say aloud, "That son of mine will never amount to a thing." By the time I extinguished my Marlboro, Jacqueline would have spoken nothing but negativity over everyone in her family and every situation in her life. As we walked out of the maintenance shop together, I usually wanted another cigarette to lift my spirits.

Long after I quit working at the day care, I still heard about Jacqueline from former coworkers. Her husband had left her for another woman. Her son had been arrested for selling drugs. She had lost nearly everything she had in a house fire. Then, most recently, I heard that Jacqueline had passed away from lung cancer.

One might think, "Poor Jacqueline. She had such a hard life. She went through so much." And that is true. I am saddened by her story. But I also know how she constantly spoke curses over her life. She believed every negative thought planted in her mind—every lie Satan dumped there—and then she spoke that junk aloud. The Bible says there is power of life or death in the tongue, and it's absolutely true.

I've been in a war with the devil. Like Jacqueline, I have foolishly believed his lies. I've been a prisoner of my own mind, and it can be downright frightening. Before I read Joyce Meyer's *Battlefield of the Mind*, there were a few times when I thought I was going crazy because of the thoughts that ran through my head. With study, research, and fervent prayer, I finally realized I didn't have to believe the devil's fabrications. I didn't have to let them control me. My brain didn't have to be his trash can.

When a thought crosses my mind that I know isn't from the

Lord or even from myself, I don't allow that disgusting seed to grow. I immediately "take it captive," as 2 Corinthians 10:5 directs me to. I cast it down in the name of Jesus, because that is the only name that makes that fallen angel cower. I purposely think on something else. I know that if I resist the devil, he will flee from me, just as James 4:7 says he will.

I hate Satan. I hate him more than Michael Scott hates Toby Flenderson. I hate that he wants to destroy not only me, but my family too. I hate that he wants to steal my joy. I hate that he prowls around with evil intent. I hate what I see him doing to our country. I hate what I see him doing to friends like Jacqueline.

I hate him, but I'm not scared of him—not in the slightest. I'm not scared that he's ticked off when I speak truth. I'm not scared of his plans. I'm not scared of any disturbing thought he tosses into my head.

Because I know Jesus.

It's similar to the commenters and social-media trolls who hate me. They can do everything in their power to tear me down. They can be overcome with rage at my beliefs or my videos or even my comedy. They can tag every friend they have (which I bet is only like two) in my posts and encourage them to put me down too. They can speak all the lies they want about me. Again, I don't care.

Because I know Jesus, what can mere human beings do to me?

That's the confidence that comes only through knowing Christ. It's a

> ✦
> I hate Satan. I hate him more than Michael Scott hates Toby Flenderson.
> ✦

peaceful, quiet confidence of knowing no matter how hated you are by this world or a social-media commenter or even Satan himself, it doesn't matter. It doesn't matter what lies pop into our minds—we don't have to believe them. We don't have to live in bondage.

Why should we believe the lies when we know the Truth?

**THINGS THAT WORK
MY NERVES #14**

Waking from a sound sleep at 3:00 a.m. to a small silhouette five inches from my face whispering, "Mama?"

There's truly nothing more frightening.
I'm surprised I haven't put my children
in a chokehold for this stunt.

Chapter Seventeen

GAS

I was in a sporting-goods store last week because softball season is quickly approaching and Natalie Ann wanted a new high-tech water bottle that has a misting feature. It's a rather genius invention—that is, unless your daughter wastes all of the water misting herself before the game and then can barely catch a ball because soaking-wet strands of hair keep falling into her eyes. That's just what I've been told anyway . . .

As we were browsing the store, I noticed a middle-class family of four apparently gearing up for a camping trip. Dad was seriously eyeballing the most expensive tent, which looked like it came complete with three bedrooms and two-and-a-half baths. Mom threw some kind of electromagnetic tennis racquet that promised to deter mosquitoes and tarantulas into the shopping cart, and the children were eager to purchase glow sticks and freeze-dried chicken a la king.

Since our family used to spend many weekends camping at a preferred spot along the Tennessee River—before the sport of softball took over our Saturdays—I knew a little about camping

and naturally had the urge to school those who weren't as experienced. I knew the cheaper tent works just as well as the Tent Mahal
(spiders still get in and crawl on your face while you sleep), the
science-fiction tennis racquet will repel a mosquito about as well
as a bloodmobile, and the chicken a la king should be reserved for
emergency situations, such as being stranded in the Alps for twelve
days. Forty-eight hours at a campsite with electricity and a pool isn't
an emergency situation, people.

(The only sensible items those happy campers had in their cart
were the glow sticks. Glow sticks are always fun—which reminds
me of the time Jason and I went to a techno club about fifteen years
ago and he got into a dance-off with some guy who juggled a dozen
glow sticks while wearing a Dr. Seuss hat. Jason lost, obviously,
probably because he wasn't on Ecstasy.)

I knew the family was purchasing many unneeded items, but
it really was none of my business. I assumed they wanted a "real"
camping experience, so I didn't say a word as they discussed which
powdered meals and flares they should purchase for their weekend
at the campground with free Wi-Fi.

When I left the camping department, I noticed a parent whose
son was about to play T-ball for the first time. Three-year-old kids
who still pee their pajamas two to five nights a week don't need
thirty-dollar batting gloves. I'm sure that boy's dad was overcome
with excitement, thinking, *This is where it begins. This is where his
professional MLB career begins*—so his little slugger needed the best
of the best. But here's the thing. One of those gloves is going to
get left in a dugout and accidentally thrown into the garbage with
a pile of Gatorade bottles, and the other is going to find its way
wedged between the third-row seats along with straw wrappers,
stale french fries, and ponytail holders, never to be seen again. That
man might as well set fire to thirty bucks. But I kept my mouth
shut and moved on.

Throughout the store that day I saw overly eager people: runners shelling out $49.99 apiece for compression shirts that could be purchased elsewhere for half price, hunters buying the most expensive doe urine when all doe urine is created equal, parents getting the best cleats for children who would probably outgrow them halfway through the season, and campers who were irrationally eager to eat freeze-dried meals. Those people reminded me of an excited schnauzer in Petco running around with its tongue hanging out while urinating in the chew-toy aisle.

I get it. So many times I've taken up a new hobby and wanted the best gear. I once decided to start swimming—like *real* swimming, not just lounging on a float with a good book—so I bought a set of high-end nose plugs and a swim cap that transformed me into Connie Conehead. I also shelled out a pretty penny on a waterproof watch with a timer and some kind of ankle weights. I didn't even know what the ankle weights were for, but I was convinced that if I wanted to win the gold, I had to have them.

I used that crap for two days before tossing it into a Rubbermaid tote and playing a game of Marco Polo with the kids. What a waste.

I did the same thing when I started running. I had a "professional" fit my feet with shoes that cost more than our patio furniture. I bought really good-looking running outfits that should only be worn by people who are already in shape. I spent a fortune on running stuff when the only thing I really needed was a good set of earbuds and an exercise bra that kept the girls in place.

When we went on a fishing trip several summers ago, I insisted on the hot-pink, Bill Dance–approved rod and reel. I didn't get so much as a bite, but my five-year-old daughter caught a bass with her Barbie pole.

And don't even get me started on the things my husband has bought for golf and hunting. There's an unused ball washer and fourteen different deer and turkey calls on my property right now.

Craigslist (and our garage) is full of stuff that was never needed in the first place: guitar amps, camera lenses, robot vacuums, metal detectors. The list goes on and on. Second mortgages have been taken out on homes just to cover the Titleist inventory in hall closets. Under Armour is no longer a brand; it's a way of life.

So many of us are sick with GAS (Gear Acquisition Syndrome). We want the latest, the greatest, and the best. We struggle with the temptation to keep shopping, and we fill our closets and our shops and attics and Pods and cousins' barns with stuff we don't really need. But all too often we are left unsatisfied and unfulfilled and wanting more, more, more.

Remember the simple days when all you needed to play ball was a bat and a glove? Remember when swimming required only a swimsuit—any kind of swimsuit? Remember when camping meant throwing a homemade tent and a bag of marshmallows in the truck?

And of course, GAS has many different (but related) variations. Even if you never enter a sporting-goods store, you may be vulnerable to FAS (Fashion Acquisition Syndrome), C-MAS (Craft Material Acquisition Syndrome), BAS (Book Acquisition Syndrome), or any number of related maladies. The inevitable result is clutter in our houses and in our lives.

There are several shows in the television lineup right now that depict a minimalist way of living. Couples reside in dwellings that resemble the playhouse my father built for me when I was five. The twelve-by-twelve building held a My Little Pony table and chairs, plastic food, and a collection of Country Crock containers my mother no longer wanted. I colored on the walls and left Play-Doh on the floor. I even had a mailbox that my mama put notes in. My father, an employee of the telephone company, rigged up a phone so I could call my mother in the kitchen. At my phone request she'd bring me Flintstone Push-Up Pops. (I loved that playhouse.)

Although I do sometimes crave a minimalist lifestyle, I don't think I could live in such a tiny space. Jason and I are both taller than the average bear, and we have two children, plus one on the way, and four dogs. It might be fun for the first few hours to sleep in a loft, shower in a broom closet, and hitch the house up to the truck anytime we want, but before long, one of us would file divorce papers.

A friend of mine often does mission work right here in America. She travels to the poorest parts of the country to help those in need. She once sent me photos of a family she visited in the Blue Ridge Mountains of West Virginia. It was like a look back to the Great Depression. The large family lived in a shack—literally a *shack*, with one-inch gaps between the clapboards and a dirt floor. The father had died young and left the mother alone to raise the children. She worked several jobs, and yet she couldn't support her large family. She took in sewing and alterations on the side just to make ends meet. Their water was muddy, their tattered clothes hung on a line, and the children were barefoot. They didn't even attend school. The pictures looked like something out of an old movie. I couldn't believe they were living in the 2000s.

"What do they need?" I asked her.

"Anything and everything," she said.

So I got to work.

I've always loved to declutter. My kids will tell you I get downright anxious when I see a messy closet. Bennett and I once had a twenty-minute negotiation over a Happy Meal toy, so I've learned my lesson. When the mood to declutter strikes, I wait until he's at school and throw every toy in my path into a bag. After the conversation with my missionary friend, I was even more on fire to clean out and donate things every few months.

For the family in West Virginia, I went through our closets and toy chests and kitchen drawers and bins in the attic. It was the first time I didn't set aside the "expensive stuff" to sell on eBay or Facebook. I threw everything, even the name-brand items and the barely used ones, into a box for her to take to that family. I'm not trying to get any praise or toot my horn, but I tell you this because I still use the image of that destitute family as motivation to declutter and find better homes for things we don't really need.

My mother was the opposite. She wasn't a hoarder with a twelve-inch path through her home and piles of empty shampoo bottles, but she did keep a lot of stuff. When she passed away we found phone books from 1987 and millions of photos that had been passed down to her from her own mother.

I don't know why Mama kept so many pictures of people she didn't even know. She even labeled them, writing things like "Unknown person, Brownsville, Tennessee, 1942" on the back of many. She hung on to letters and birthday cards and several "power suits" with shoulder pads from the eighties. She never went to a Halloween party as Murphy Brown, so I don't know why she allowed those suits to take up several cubic feet in her closet.

Mama also held on to every picture my siblings, Keith and Carmen, and I ever drew—every report card, every program from church, piles of newspaper clippings, and other things she deemed sentimental. I did not inherit this trait from my mother. This is going to sound cruel, but unless that picture my kid drew is "refrigerator worthy," it's going in the garbage. If I kept their every doodle, my house would look like a landfill.

My husband, on the other hand, is more like a male version of Mama. We're going to build a workshop on our property one day, Lord willing and the creek don't rise, but for now our garage is full of Jason's stuff—and I do mean full, mostly of stuff we have no real use for. We do need the lawnmower and a place to park his 1971 Ford Bronco. We also need Jason's workbench and tools. But do we really need the propane heater that he, his brother, and his mother used to boil eggs for tuna-fish salad during the ice-storm power outage of 1994? I mean, we already have several propane heaters. Is he expecting another ice age?

I look around that garage and don't know what half of the stuff does because I've never seen Jason use it. He's not into woodworking or forging knives, so I don't understand why he has the equipment to do both. And someone please tell me why he's kept every license plate he's ever had? Is he planning to open a Cracker Barrel?

I'm reminded of a verse in Luke that reads, "Watch out! Be on your guard against all kinds of greed; life does not consist in an abundance of possessions" (Luke 12:15). I'm not saying my husband or my mother are greedy! Not at all. But sometimes I wonder if there's the tiniest bit of idolatry involved in keeping all that stuff.

Even items with real sentimental value can get to be too much. At one time, for instance, Natalie had roughly seventy-five trophies on her dresser. Each one represented an accolade, a symbol of achievement. She clutched them tightly in the back seat on the way home from a pageant, a softball tournament, or a school function. We proudly displayed them. They provided some temporary joy. But after a while they were just dust magnets. Clutter. We eventually packed them into boxes and put them in the attic.

I'm reminded of those verses in Matthew 5 about moths and rust. (I always thought Moth and Rust would be a fantastic heavy-metal band name.) We store up treasures here on earth and have every right to be proud of them and the hard work and perseverance associated with them, but eventually they lose their appeal. They have absolutely nothing to do with what really matters. They are temporary and susceptible to moths and rust and other kinds of decay.

Don't get me wrong—I do have several boxes of "special" things. This is to be expected when both of your parents are dead. I still have one of my dad's shirts hanging in my closet. It's been there for over twenty years. I don't know if I'll ever be able to let it go. I have my mother's bathrobe, stained with dollops of her hair color, and her Bible and several things she left specifically for me. Right after she passed away, I could barely throw away those photos of people even she didn't know because they had rested in her armoire for so long, but as time went on, I was able to get rid of a lot of things that didn't really matter much to me.

> We aren't to cling to the newest devices and dozens of pairs of shoes and gadgets and the best of the best or the awards we've received here on earth. We are to cling to what is eternal.

I really do believe we aren't meant to cling to things. We aren't to cling to the newest devices and dozens of pairs of shoes and gadgets and the best of the best or the awards we've received here on earth. We are to cling to what is eternal. The solid rock. Christ alone. That's where our self-worth is really found.

And can't no moth touch it.

**THINGS THAT WORK
MY NERVES #214**

*When they rearrange
my grocery store*

As soon as I learn the layout, someone moves
everything around, and then there's a box of
tampons where the Pop-Tarts used to be. I don't
need this kind of added stress in my life.

Chapter Eighteen

Lose Your Pride

Remember a few chapters back when I talked about Bennett's attitude when he was addicted to video games? He was angry a lot in those days—defiant even. But at that time I hadn't yet made the connection between the games and the attitude. It hadn't yet occurred to me that the enemies he'd been shooting on his screen—and the addictive nature of the gaming itself—probably influenced him.

One particular school night after a video-game binge, he started acting especially ugly. He was mad he had to turn off the PlayStation. He was mad he had to go to school in the morning. He was mad that Pepper had chewed up his Steph Curry socks. He was just downright mad.

I often think of the saying "He's not giving you a hard time. He's having a hard time." So, instead of fueling the fire by yelling at him, I loved on him and hugged him. It didn't work. He just wanted to be mad. He crossed his arms and huffed and puffed. I told him to go to sleep and that everything would be better tomorrow.

"Son, go to bed," I said when he appeared in the kitchen ten minutes after I had tucked him in.

He just stood there, mad.

"Son, go to bed," I repeated.

He just stood there, mad.

"Boy, get in the bed now!" I demanded in, well, a different voice. I'm really nice the first two times I say something, but if I have to say it a third time, I tend to turn green, sprout muscles, and bust my blue jeans.

Bennett still just stood there, which is really odd because going Hulk usually works.

So I calmly said, "I know you're in a bad mood, but now you are letting your anger control you, and you are disobeying. It's past your bedtime. Go to bed."

"No."

Straight defiance, y'all.

"What did you say?" I refrained from gritting my teeth and tossing him up the stairs by the back of his pajama shirt.

"I don't want to go to bed."

In our home, time-out isn't an option for defiance and back-talk, so I said, "I'm giving you one last chance to turn around, go upstairs, and get in your bed. If you don't I'm getting the belt because you are disobeying."

(Insert record scratch sound here.)

Let's take this opportunity to piggyback onto another topic that is worthy of a good rant—spanking. I don't care if you believe in spanking or not. I don't care what methods you use to discipline your children. You do what you need to do. You do what *you* believe in, what works for your family. However, Jason and I discipline our children the same way we were disciplined—and we don't need anyone's blessing in the matter.

My precious Granny Rebecca used to make me get my own

switch from a tree in her backyard when I back-talked or disobeyed her. And let me tell you, I deserved every spanking she ever gave me. She never abused me. She didn't scar me for life. Instead, she taught me that lack of respect and poor decisions have consequences.

I mentioned spanking in a blog post one time and received a ton of nasty e-mails on the matter. I paid them no mind, but I wish I could have heard my grandmother's response to them. I think she would have said something like, "Darlin', sounds to me like they need to get their own switch."

Now, where were we? Oh, yeah. Bennett was being a real brat at bedtime. He stood firm when I threatened him with the belt, so I kept my word. Jason was not at home, but I retrieved that strap of brown leather from his closet and popped my little boy on the butt with it three times.

He stood there rubbing his butt cheek as tears rolled down his face. I knelt down on his level and told him, "You've acted very ugly tonight and have been punished for it. Now, are you ready to make it right?"

He remained silent, with his arms tightly crossed.

"Are you going to apologize for your behavior?"

He just stood there, his face hardened and his lips pursed.

"They are really easy words to say. And when you say them— and mean them—you know that everything will immediately be better."

"They *aren't* easy words," he mumbled.

As I knelt there in our kitchen, face-to-face with my son, he reminded me so much of me. Those crossed arms. That rigid face, so full of pride. He would rather be bitter and angry than admit he was wrong.

"Okay, then," I said. "Go on upstairs and get in the bed."

Not wanting another pop on his bottom, he turned around and walked away in his Batman boxers.

More times than I can count in my thirty-seven years, I've behaved that way. I've been too proud to admit my wrong actions to family and friends. The words have been too difficult to say. And more times than I care to admit, I've acted that way to my Lord too.

Just as Bennett pushed away from me, I've pushed away from God. I was too haughty to admit that I'd sinned, too proud to admit my faults and humble myself before Him. I just couldn't bring myself to say, "Lord, I messed up, and I'm sorry. God, I humble myself before You because I know I can do nothing apart from You."

I've seen it in others, too—standing there with hardened faces and hardened hearts, arms tightly crossed. While He lovingly looks on and gives every chance to repent, we remain stubborn. We allow anger and resentment to fester. We allow guilt to press down on us and rob us of joy. We are arrogant and foolish.

Sometimes I'm punished for that behavior, just as Bennett was spanked with the belt. Our God is a loving God, of course, but I believe He does punish our bad attitudes and behavior. (I've certainly encountered pain and punishment as a result of my actions.) We may be punished by losing a job or losing a relationship or just being so disconnected from God that nothing seems to go right, and His jerking a knot in our tails is the very thing we need to see the error of our ways.

That night I wanted nothing more than for Bennett to say to me, "Mama, I'm sorry." I wanted him to say the words so the tension could immediately cease. I wanted him to say the words and for peace to flood our home. I wanted him to say the words so I could scoop him into my arms.

But he wouldn't say them. Instead, he chose to turn around and walk away.

I went to check on him a few minutes later, and he was finally asleep. His pillow was damp from tears. I wiped his face, stroked his hair. I bent down to kiss his sweet cheek and whispered to him, "I love you, my boy."

Bennett didn't say he was sorry that evening, but I loved him anyway. He misbehaved, but I loved him anyway. I still wiped his tears and kissed his cheek. And when he did apologize the next day, with a convicted heart and tears of remorse, I was there with open arms.

> **If we love our children with that kind of unconditional love, how much more does our Father love us?**

If we love our children with that kind of unconditional love, how much more does our Father love us?

God longs for our repentance. He longs for it the same way I longed for my son to apologize to me. Even when we don't, His love doesn't falter. But how much better our lives will be if we uncross our arms and release the pride in our hearts.

Try it. Say the words. Mean them.

Then welcome the peace and wisdom that comes with humility.

**THINGS THAT WORK
MY NERVES #59**

Mold

Why do I only notice the green growth on the
bread after I've eaten half the sandwich?

Chapter Nineteen

No Cookie for You

Like any loving mother, I'm incredibly proud of my children.

I'm proud of their manners, their kind hearts, their willingness to share with other children and not act like jerks 99.7 percent of the time. I'm proud of their beauty—on the outside *and* the inside. I'm proud of their intelligent minds and sharp senses of humor.

I'm also proud of their talents. They both excel in different sports and have amazing artistic abilities. Natalie Ann is only in junior high, but she has a God-given talent for the piano. My mother, an incredibly talented pianist, showed Natalie a few chords when she was just a toddler in Pull-Ups, and she took to the keyboard like a duck to water. I never fail to think of my mother every time my girl sits on the piano bench. When she effortlessly plays some classical piece of music, tears of pride stream down my cheeks. (And she usually says, "Oh, gosh, Mama. Get it together.")

My sweet boy, too, is one of the brightest lights in my life. I love his sensitivity and empathy. I love how he worries about others and cares so deeply for his dogs. I love that he's the kind kid, the accepting kid, the humble kid. I love the smile on his face when he catches a fish, aces a test, or storms down a basketball court without double dribbling. I love that he is mine.

At this writing, our Annabeth is still just a cantaloupe in my womb (and the source of horrible heartburn), but I know she'll bring me to tears with her acts of kindness and talent as well. I can't wait to see all her accomplishments.

Although my children easily shine in many areas, however, they struggle in others. Some things just don't come naturally to them. And in those areas, while I don't necessarily expect them to be the best, I do expect them to work and do their best.

I'm willing to help. I've cheered them on as they worked their butts off to achieve goals, both academically and athletically. I've hauled them all over God's green country to practices and rehearsals. I've quizzed them on notes and held up flash cards. On the way to school in the morning, we've said prayers for nervousness to cease and for minds to be sharp and for answers to be remembered.

Usually, of course, they take it upon themselves to work hard and prepare for whatever comes their way. But I've also watched them slack off and become sluggish in practice and preparation, then wonder why they failed the test or missed the goal or played the wrong note. And when that happens, I am not one of those parents who showers them with praise and treats. I just don't believe that lackluster work or lack of effort should be rewarded.

I'll never forget when Natalie Ann played horribly in a third-grade basketball game. She was so busy chewing her nails and fiddling with her hair that she let several balls dribble right past her. I know, I know—she was only eight at the time. But she was usually an aggressive player even at such a young age, and that day she just wasn't into the game. I was sorely disappointed to watch her slowly shuffle down the court as if she had somewhere better to be.

When Natalie walked off the court after the game (without a single bead of sweat on her forehead), my mother was there waiting with open arms to shower her with "good job" and pats on the back. And that, quite frankly, made me angry. Most times Natalie Ann deserved applause. She has always been a hardworking and determined kid who can do anything she puts her mind to. But that day she did not deserve to be doted on. Her grandmother was lying to her. She *hadn't* done a good job.

"Mama," I said when Natalie was out of earshot. "She played terribly. She was more focused when she played ball in kindergarten."

"She's only eight, Susannah. You're too hard on her."

"I don't expect her to shoot a three-pointer, but I do expect her to run instead of walk and not braid her hair on the court."

I remember, too, when Bennett threw a fit during a singing program in pre-K. I don't recall the specifics, but he crossed his arms and refused to sing the song about summer vacation. He just stood there looking like a little Gymboree model who had sucked a dang lemon. After the show my mama was there. "Oh, you did so good, sweet boy! So good!"

"Did so good at what, Mama? Sucking lemons?"

Mama also praised everything I did as a child even when I didn't give 100 percent. After every mucked-up piano recital or lost basketball game or failed test, she droned on and on about how well I had performed. Despite what she said, I knew I hadn't done well. I was completely capable of making a free throw or flawlessly playing a piano piece I'd learned or acing a biology exam—if I practiced or studied, that is. But when I hadn't prepared, it was always evident. I often didn't deserve her praise, and over time her always-adoring attitude skewed my thinking. I didn't believe I had to work hard because everything I did, no matter how poorly, was good enough for Mommy.

During my school years I often let coaches and teammates down because of my laziness. I was kicked out of academic clubs.

Unfortunately that superior attitude of, "I'm amazing at everything" stuck with me throughout college. I learned really quickly, from professors with stern voices and cold eyes, that I was not the bee's knees. Without effort and hard work, I was mediocre at best.

Don't misunderstand me. I'm so grateful I had a mother who never let me forget how loved and precious I was to her. But as I grew older, I realized she'd been too easy on me during my adolescence. I'm sure she felt sorry for me because Daddy had died in my presence when I was so young. But her coddling meant that other people in this world had to be responsible for letting me know that poor work would not be rewarded.

What I really needed to hear from my mom after any subpar performance was, "I know what you are capable of doing, and I didn't see that today. You didn't give it your best. If you practice really hard, I know you'll do better next time. Hard work always pays off. You can do better."

Maybe my feelings would have been hurt. Maybe I would've rolled my eyes and sighed. But maybe I also would have practiced my butt off and been an asset to my team at the next game. Maybe I even would've made it to Juilliard or the WNBA.

Even worse than the parent praising lack of effort is the parent who insists their child can do no wrong. My mother was that way to an extent. I was a little heathen at times and got in trouble at school for talking out of turn or being sarcastic. And when Mama was called to the school, she usually defended me, insisting that I didn't mean any harm or that calling her hadn't been necessary. (Except for the one time I got a paddling at school for writing a really rude note about a teacher I loathed, and she tore up my backside with a hairbrush when I got home too. I still flinch at the sight of a wooden brush.)

As parents, we want to believe the best concerning our children. But if you show me evidence that my darlings have misbehaved, they will be punished—not defended and coddled.

I know several parents who commend every move their children make, but one woman in particular makes me madder than a wet hen. I guess she means well, bless her heart, but sometimes I want to interrupt her over-the-top praise and say, "Have you seen the stuff your little Tiffany posts on Instagram? And I watched her beat up another kid at the park right before robbing an old lady at gunpoint. Tiffany can be lower than a snake's belly in a wagon rut. Please quit pretending she's all rainbows and sprinkles and holier than thou." Little Tiffany is a brat, plain and simple. And her mother's refusal to see her true behavior and discipline her is a crying shame.

Sports parents are the worst about bragging on their kids. I had a conversation at a softball tournament with a woman who called her child a prodigy. Repeatedly. "Babette Ruth" is only eight, Danielle. Let's not call in the college recruiters just yet. At least wait until she finishes eating her Ring Pop in the outfield before getting ESPN on the line.

And if the future softball World Series pitcher throws eighteen balls in a row, there's always a plethora of excuses. Danielle paces around the bleachers telling all the parents, "She didn't warm up. She was up late last night. She forgot to take her steroids this morning." I'd love to hear Danielle say instead, "She's only eight and still wets the bed. No one expects her to throw a seventy-three-miles-per-hour screwball."

It's great that Danielle is proud of her daughter and thinks so highly of her. My children know how proud Jason and I are of them. And I don't want my lack of praise to be confused with abuse. I don't tell my kids they suck. I always offer encouragement when they are down. When I know they've put in hard work and still haven't succeeded, we talk about not giving up and about knowing their worth in Christ. I remind them that they are chosen according to the purpose of God—and that purpose may not always be an athletic scholarship or gold medal.

Thinking back to that elementary basketball game so many years ago, if Natalie Ann had been aggressive instead of chewing her cuticles and she'd still failed to stop the ball or make a layup, I would not have been disappointed. She'd have gotten her pat on the back and her cookie. And if Bennett had stuck his lip back in and just sung the darn song about sunglasses and summer vacation—even off key—I'd have kissed all over his fat little cheeks and told him he'd done great.

> I don't believe that loving children means you must constantly praise them. I'll never let them believe that failing to give it all they've got is okay.

I'm not over here locking kids in closets because they missed a pop fly or struck out at the plate. I'm not whipping them with piano wire and drumsticks. However, I don't believe that loving children means you must constantly praise them. I'll never let them believe that failing to give it all they've got is okay. They'll never be told by me that they are entitled to anything.

It's not about winning.

It's about giving it your all.

**THINGS THAT WORK
MY NERVES #32**

Powdered sugar

When my kids walk around the house with a bag
of Donettes, I'm left to clean up more white
powder than Pablo Escobar's maid.

Chapter Twenty

Maybe It's Your Fault

"It's not my fault!"

Do your children say that when they get into trouble? Mine often do. They blame each other. They blame a friend. They blame the dogs. They blame the Elf on the Shelf. But I'm not having it. As soon as they utter the words, I lapse into a spiel about taking responsibility for their actions.

"It is not Tucker's fault that your shoes have been chewed to shreds. How many times did I tell you to bring them inside? He got tired of those smelly Crocs sitting beside his doghouse for three days and had to destroy them! Can you blame him?"

I can scroll through my social media feeds right now and I guarantee I will see a post written by someone who does not make a big deal about taking responsibility. Posters like that, usually women, love to blame others. Oh, they can go on and on until the cows come home. I read a vent the other night about what was lacking in one gal's marriage. She spoke of all the things her husband needed to do and the changes he needed to make, but she never once mentioned herself. She never took blame.

This is the very kind of woman who always blames other women too. It's never her fault when a friendship falls apart, is it? She even blames her children—for her wine addiction and her mental breakdown and even for the fact that she didn't fulfill her lifelong dream of backpacking across Europe before getting pregnant. (Yes, I've actually read posts that insinuate this.) When someone posts her business all over Facebook, I want so badly to reply, "Maybe *you're* the reason you can't keep friends or have a happy marriage." But of course, I don't. I just unfollow her and move on with my life.

Let's give this woman a specific name to keep things simple. Trisha, the drama queen, would be an excellent leading lady in a soap opera. She would do a fine job of gazing bewildered into a camera before a commercial break. She throws adult temper tantrums and sweats the small stuff and doesn't know how to pick battles in her friendships, her marriage, and her role as a mother.

Trisha is also a bossy nag. She constantly tells her friends and children and husband, Darren, what to do. (We should absolutely instruct and steer our kids, but there's nothing worse than a mother who constantly badgers her children. Women like Trisha have no clue how to relinquish control.) Trisha constantly complains and criticizes and condemns Darren and every other person who doesn't live up to her expectations. Her reminders and requests are nothing but the ugly and annoying noise of a broken record. Trisha doesn't have a clue how to communicate in an appreciative and loving way.

Trisha's main form of communication is Facebook. She often (hourly) gives intricate details of every dramatic incident that goes on in her family:

> Darren was arrested yesterday afternoon for spray-painting graffiti on railroad cars at the depot downtown. He was detained by Jamie Reeves, a deputy of the Thompson County Sheriff's Department. He had an active warrant for his arrest because he stole the T-tops off his uncle Harvey's Pontiac Trans Am in 2004. Well, I was

getting a bikini wax down at Curl Up 'n' Dye when Darren had the audacity to call me from the sheriff's office and ask me to post his bail. I seriously could not believe it. I am not about to bail out the man who has put me through so much stress over these last few months. He is scheduled to see Judge McJudy at 10:15 Thursday morning. I hope she puts him under the jail—with Darren Davis.

Hold your horses, Trisha.

Did you really just tag Darren in the Facebook status where you told all his business? And did you conveniently leave out the fact that you drove Darren so crazy with your nagging and drama that his stress reliever is spray-painting graffiti on railroad cars? Also, you know good and well he stole those T-tops at your request because you've had it out for Uncle Harvey ever since he only gave you a 3 percent tip when you waitressed at the truck stop.

Even when the police aren't involved, Trisha doesn't know how to properly connect with poor Darren. He's not charging $2.99 per minute to tell fortunes over the telephone, so he doesn't know Trisha had a horrible day and wants him to bring home dinner. He can't read her thoughts, and she can't read his, no matter how hard she stares at him with those squinted eyes. She should tell the man what she wants and needs (not on social media) and expect the same from him. Assuming Darren knows Trisha's every wish is just gearing her up for a nagging episode when he doesn't deliver. So she goes at it again on Facebook:

> Darren came home after work and asked what was for supper. I gave him a bowl of Cap'n Crunch, and now he's on the couch watching baseball. Doesn't he know the ferret has had diarrhea *all day* and I've had to clean its cage over two hundred times? Doesn't he realize I'm exhausted after looking for deals on Rakuten all day? Doesn't Darren know I've had such a busy day that I didn't get a chance to go to the grocery store? Ugh! Men!

No, Trisha. Darren doesn't know. Here's an idea: why don't you tell him?

Poor Trisha has no concept of forgiving and forgetting either. She won't let Harvey's pitiful tip go. She'll never let poor Darren forget the time he accidentally set fire to the couch. Because her high school friend Jenny never returned her Shania Twain CD, she refuses to accept her friend request on Facebook (lucky for Jenny).

Let it go, Trisha. The good Lord expects you to.

The bottom line is, Trisha is immature. Her tantrums and nagging and refusal to apologize and accept apologies are the problem. She's bossy and nosy and is logged into her social media accounts entirely too often. She's to blame for the strife, and the sooner Trisha grows up, the happier everyone in her life (and news feed) will be.

Now. A question.

Are you Trisha?

Reread it, sister. Flip back and see if you sound anything like this woman.

I admit it: while I was writing this, I recognized hints of myself. I don't post on Facebook every time Jason is arrested for spray-painting property, but I'm guilty of the nagging and the bossiness from time to time. I'm guilty of expecting Jason to know what I need without telling him. I'm guilty of holding on to grudges and being dramatic. I'm guilty of stirring the pot.

I'm wrong about something or another every single day. And I can't place the blame on anyone but me.

Like Trisha, I will not be perfect until I reach the other side of heaven. So while I'm here on earth, I've got to own up to my many wrongs and apologize for them. You do too, sister. It's not always someone else's fault. The quicker you, me, and Trisha own up and stop putting unneeded stress on the foundations of our relationships, the happier everyone is going to be.

THINGS THAT WORK
MY NERVES #83

Dog duty (doody)

They say having a puppy is like having a baby,
but I've never had to take my child outside
at 2:00 a.m. and wait for it to poop.

Chapter Twenty-One ✦

Talk and Walk

✦

I've never been one to comfortably talk about stuff like copulation. I've been married for fourteen years, and I still blush at the very idea. In fact, I only copulate on Christmas and Jason's birthday—which explains why I get so depressed around the holidays.

That last part is a joke. Jason's birthday isn't even close to Christmas.

However, it's no joke that I've never been one to talk about such acts. I mean, I'm a thirty-seven-year-old woman who'd rather use the word *copulation* than *sex*. I was raised by a mama who told me S-E-X is a private affair, sacred between husband and wife, so I don't dig all this copulation talk on television and movies and the Copulation station on Pandora. (They play a lot of Barry White.)

In fact, I'm now rethinking the story I'm about to tell you because I will have to read it in front of people when I record the audiobook. I'll need to apply extra deodorant and up my Lexapro dosage.

But here goes.

Several years ago Jason and I needed some "kid free" time, so I channeled my inner romantic and concocted a wonderful plan to kidnap my husband and stow away to a cabin in the beautiful Ozark Mountains for the weekend. I searched for cabins on the internet, and every single one had *copulation* written all over it. The following description is real:

> Beautiful mountain view. Watch deer from the back porch and squirrels nesting in the majestic pines. Let all of your cares drift away in this gorgeous country cabin. Amenities include king-sized bed, jacuzzi tub, coffeemaker, eight-foot brass dance pole, and flat-screen television.

Say what, now? Eight-foot brass dance pole? Right there, nestled between the coffeemaker and LCD television, the website casually mentions a brass dance pole. "Watch the deer. Watch the squirrels. Put on some tassels, crank up Guns N' Roses' 'Welcome to the Jungle,' and throw your leg around a pole." Amenities did not include Clorox wipes and antibiotics, so I stifled the vomit threatening to escape and continued my search.

I finally found the perfect place for our weekend getaway. Picture a beautiful log cabin with a wraparound porch and tin roof. Inside it was wonderfully cozy and beautifully decorated like a ski lodge. Looking down at the living area from the loft made you want to wear fur-lined Ugg boots and curl up on a bearskin rug next to the crackling fire and sip cocoa.

There was no pole next to the coffeemaker, but it was still evident that couples came to this cabin to copulate. Whirlpool tub for two. Track lighting. Hot tub on the back porch. Mirrors. And various signs posted around the room with instructions like, "Do not lean against this shelf. It will break." "Do not bear weight on this table. It will break." "You will be charged for any stained towels." "Do not lean on loft railing. It will break. You will fall twenty-five feet. You will die. Naked."

As soon as Jason entered the front door with our suitcases in hand, he said, "Woo! People have been getting busy up in here!"

"Don't even talk about it, Jason!" I shuddered and exclaimed to my longtime husband.

The owners of the cabin, two octogenarians named Herbert and Doreen, stopped by on their golf cart to welcome us. Herbert wore a brown cardigan sweater and elastic-waist pants and mall-walker shoes. Doreen had a precious visor nestled in her gray curls, wore a tidy blouse tucked into her denim slacks, and also wore mall-walker shoes.

"I just put fresh water in the hot tub, dear." Herb winked at me as if he knew the last vacationers had copulated in the tub and he expected my husband and me to do the same.

"You kids have a good time." Doreen winked at me as if she knew the last vacationers had copulated all weekend and she expected my husband and me to do the same.

Shivers ran down my spine. I understand sex is a natural part of life. It was created by God. It's what we are supposed to do with our spouses. It's the reason I have children. Duh. I get it. But I'm still embarrassed that an elderly couple assumed I was about to do that very thing with my husband in a cabin in the woods. I don't want a man named Herbert in a brown cardigan to talk about hot-tub water and give me a wink before he pulls away in an E-Z-GO. The end.

Yes, "the end." I won't go into detail about our weekend. However, I will say that the front porch of the cabin was the perfect place to finish reading *The Guernsey Literary and Potato Peel Pie Society* while Jason took a nap.

This story is about as raunchy as I get.

I'll never forget being at a sleepover in eighth grade when a friend told a filthy joke riddled with awful language. It made me uncomfortable. It didn't agree with my spirit at all, and it made my pretty, innocent friend seem ugly and crude. It wasn't as if I'd never heard cussing. My mother (yes, the church pianist and most godly woman I ever knew) had her favorite four-letter words, which she used when she broke a glass or dented the car in the grocery store parking lot, but she never said anything terribly vulgar like my friend did at the party that evening.

Not long after that party, though, I was letting the expletives fly. I could barely complete a sentence without including one. I was one of the foulest-mouthed kids in high school. Even when Jason and I started dating, he made the comment, "You're too pretty to use that kind of language."

I didn't care. I told him to shut the you-know-what up, and then I lit a cigarette. Yes, I had become a real classy broad. (Thank You, Jesus, for unconditional love and mercy.) I wrote like I spoke too. I've deleted dozens of old blog posts because they were riddled with such awful language.

I was never convicted by my language until I drew closer to the Lord after Mama died. I experienced so much spiritual growth at that time, and He started calling me to share my testimony of restoration with others. He also kept placing this verse on my heart:

> Let the words of my mouth
> and the meditation of my heart
> Be acceptable in Your sight,
> O Lord. (Ps. 19:14 NASB)

I had never thought my potty mouth was a big deal. I even had that "I love Jesus but I cuss a little" shirt and wore it with pride. But now, suddenly, talking that way seemed like a sin to me. I knew I couldn't stand on a stage as Christ's representative and then drop the f-bomb as soon as I got to the parking lot.

Now, I am not going to lie. I still struggle with keeping my talk pure. Oh mercy, yes. I slip up. When I'm trying to retrieve a piping-hot casserole from the oven and I drop it to the floor, my first instinct isn't to say, "Oh golly gee." But I'm better today than I was yesterday, thank God. That's what growing in our spirituality is all about—we are becoming new creations.

Even back when I cussed like a sailor, I still refrained from talking publicly about intimate or personal stuff like, yes, copulation. That just made me uncomfortable. It still does. But I can think of several internet mommies with incredibly large platforms who are always posting and saying things that make this Southern Baptist cringe. I'm not a pearl clutcher by any means, but some of the talk I've heard coming out of petite, well-dressed women sitting in their gourmet kitchens with pot fillers in the background have made me want to clutch, baby, clutch! And bathe, baby, bathe! I don't need to hear every detail of their Pap smear or sex life or toilet time. That may be what gets them a laugh from others, but it gets an "ugh" from me.

> I'm not a pearl clutcher by any means, but some of the talk I've heard coming out of petite, well-dressed women sitting in their gourmet kitchens with pot fillers in the background have made me want to clutch, baby, clutch!

This is a perfect opportunity to call me judgmental. It's fine. I won't take the time to defend myself. You can throw that adjective around all you want if you're referencing me trying to please the Lord instead of man. I was saved for years before I was ever convicted of talking like Andrew Dice Clay, so I cannot cast a stone, but once God told me to simmer down, I knew my speech wasn't pleasing to Him. So maybe those blogger ladies who speak that way are still where I used to be. If they know Christ, they'll get that nudge from the Holy Spirit to replace the profanity with praises. And then, bless their hearts, they will spend an entire Saturday deleting blog posts and videos the way I did.

It's not just the words we say or the topics we discuss, of course. What do the photos of us on social media portray? Are we flipping the bird in a picture the day after we posted a Bible verse? Are we hanging out with people who hurt our witness? If we are followers of Christ, is it evident to those around us? We can sit alone in our prayer closets all night, but how do we behave when others are watching? Are we a stumbling block for our brothers and sisters?

I used to proclaim how good God was and then be tagged in a photo on Myspace with a shot of Jägermeister in my hand. It didn't add up because a person cannot serve two masters. We are called to practice what we preach.

When I was asked to teach middle-school girls at church on Sunday mornings, I had to sign a waiver stating I would walk the talk. It would be hypocritical for me to mentor young and impressionable children of God on Sunday morning and then be seen on Instagram half drunk another day of the week. Before I signed the waiver, I spoke with a leader in our church. I told him I was no longer a heavy drinker like I used to be, but I occasionally had a margarita on my back porch in the summer. I enjoyed a mojito on the white, sandy beaches of Key West. A glass of red wine paired well with frozen pizza. I no longer drank to get drunk, but was I fit to teach those sweet girls?

The leader I spoke with said that he appreciated my honesty, that several had signed that waiver and continued to live their lives however they wanted. He also said he couldn't tell me to sign it or not—that was between me and the Lord. But the fact that God had prompted me to bring the matter to him instead of just sign-ing the waiver meant something. It meant I took God's conviction seriously. I wanted to please Him. And that is the main goal of a Christian mentor.

I've prayed over the situation often and have yet to be convicted if I have a frosty Blue Moon with a slice of orange on the privacy of my back porch on a hot, summer night; therefore I don't consider my drinking a sin. My father couldn't do that though. After he went to rehab for alcohol, he could not have even a sip of alcohol. He could not sit on the porch and only have one beer. It was impossible for him. Two drinks would turn into twelve. Praise the Lord, I don't face that struggle.

This isn't me trying to justify my sin. The moment God says to me, "That doesn't please Me, Susannah," I'll throw that Blue Moon in the garbage and won't look back. I'm listening for His voice.

What is He telling you? Is He nudging you to step away from certain habits and behaviors? Is He calling you to go further with Him—to give up things that others may deem harmless? What is He specifically asking you to do? What does He want you to deny? What cross does He want you to take up? Is He calling you to become a new creation?

And are you listening?

THINGS THAT WORK
MY NERVES #18

Being sick in the bed for two days

When I finally exit my bedroom, I discover the
rest of the house looks like the hotel room
in *Fear and Loathing in Las Vegas*.

Chapter Twenty-Two

Thrives on Neglect

My mother's thumb was green as grass. Yes, she had a fungus under her thumbnail for several years after getting a manicure at Happy Nail, but that's not what I'm speaking of. Mama was a wonderful gardener. The flower beds surrounding our cypress-wood house were gorgeous and led to our grounds being chosen as "Yard of the Month" by our hometown newspaper. Colorful hydrangeas and impatiens spilled over the flower-bed border and onto the sidewalk that led to our front porch, which was crowded with large terra-cotta pots filled with purple and pink petals. The clematis that climbed our mailbox post was so breathtaking that drivers often stopped their cars in the middle of the street to admire it.

Mama was also a talented florist. She often picked fresh flowers from our beds and arranged them beautifully in the large vase that sat atop her baby grand piano. She'd incorporate stems into the homemade wreaths that hung on every door to our house.

Looking back, I took for granted the natural beauty that surrounded our home. I did inherit her love for plants and flowers though. I'll never forget the first spring after she died, when I sat in the mulch of my own flower bed and cried over my hostas. Filling my pots with annuals that year felt lonely. Working in the dirt with her had been one of my favorite parts of life.

I didn't give up on gardening though. And these days, instead of loneliness, it gives me a sense of connection with Mama. I love to dig, prune, even weed. And a trip to the greenhouse or garden center makes me feel like a kid in a candy store.

When I was at the greenhouse one afternoon, I spotted a plant with a tag on it that read "thrives on neglect." My first thought was, "What an awesome band name!" I could just hear Natalie saying, "Mama, Kate just scored tickets to Thrives on Neglect this weekend. Can I go?" Then I thought a little more about that tag, and it made me think about some people I've met.

Plants that thrive on neglect do just that—they are fine if you forget to water them for a while. You don't have to worry about singing or talking to them either. Not that I sing and talk to my plants all that often. But the term for those neglected plants also reminds me of certain people. You know, folks who seem to thrive on neglect—to get something out of being treated poorly, having hard times, and being the victim.

When I think about defining moments in my life, I always include the deaths of my father, mother, and godfather. I was an orphan before the age of thirty-five, and because writing is so cathartic for me, I've written in great detail on my blog and in articles about the grief and sorrow associated with their passing. But one thing I have always worried about when writing about these losses is giving the impression that I am, or want to be perceived as, a victim. I've never coveted pity, yet I feel I may get it when I talk about losing the people I loved.

I'm a victor, not a victim. Crappy things have happened to me, but that's par for the course for everyone in this fallen world. I often think of Paul's trials and tribulations. *Bless his heart.* He had it pretty rough, but he chose victory in Jesus over being a victim. Those who thrive on neglect believe the opposite.

The gist of my testimony is this: God works every storm for our good. He gives us beauty for ashes and rainbows for lightning. Faith in Him makes all the difference. It's what makes us victors instead of victims. It's what makes the orphan a son or daughter.

It is written in Proverbs 10:25,

> When the storm has swept by, the wicked are gone,
> but the righteous stand firm forever.

This verse assures us that, in God's perfect timing, the storms of life will come to an end and there will be no more wickedness . . . *but.* There's a big, fat (sorry for using the forbidden f-word again), important *but* . . .

But the *righteous* stand firm forever.

Our society doesn't like to exclude anyone. Exclusion gives people hissy fits. Exclusion prompts the use of words that grind my gears—words like *judgmental* and *offended.* And yet the Bible is firm that not everyone is promised what the righteous are promised. Not everyone is blessed through their storms. Not everyone finds relief amid the whirlwind. Not everyone gets the rainbow. Only the righteous are given grace and mercy and purpose through trials. Only the righteous will still be standing when everything is over.

So who in the world is righteous?

My boy Webster says *righteous* means morally right or justifiable, virtuous, good, or excellent.

Those certainly aren't the adjectives I use to describe myself. It's only 9:00 a.m., and I've already been the opposite of virtuous. I had a terrible thought about someone I was watching on television, and

I've already plotted to kill the raccoon that tore open our garbage last night.

I'm far from righteous. We all are. The standard is Jesus, and it's impossible for any human to be as morally right, virtuous, good, or excellent as He is.

There's good news though. True righteousness for us humans is possible only through the cleansing of sin by Jesus. According to 2 Corinthians 5:21, "God made him who had no sin to be sin for us, so that in him we might become the righteousness of God."

At Calvary, Christ died on the cross and exchanged our sin for His perfect righteousness so we can one day blamelessly stand before God. Instead of seeing all the wretched things we've done, God will find us innocent and only see the holy righteousness given to us by what Jesus did on the cross. When we accept what Jesus did, humble ourselves before Him, and admit we can do nothing apart from Him, *then* we are considered righteous. Only then are we promised that we will stand firm forever.

Those who refuse to believe in Jesus aren't promised that. I'm just going to go ahead and say it—they are excluded.

People who thrive on neglect (or are content and "in their element" with neglect) seem to have one storm after the other, with no relief in sight. They prove bitter and mad at the world and everyone in it. They exhaust themselves (and family and friends) by attempting to fight storm after storm, only to be pelted with more wind and rain. They are miserable. They are lost. They don't know how to function without drama. And yet, they relish in being a victim and in self-sabotage and the attention associated with it.

Of course, Christians have bad days. We can certainly be depressed and downtrodden. But to truly know Christ is to have access to the fruits of the Holy Spirit—one of those being joy. I don't think it's possible to be downtrodden and miserable all of the time—to consider yourself a victim and thrive on neglect—if you know Jesus. It's an oxymoron.

It's so important that those of us made blameless through our belief in Christ share the good news with our lost brothers and sisters—those who see more storms than Jim Cantore. We are commissioned, as the hands and feet of Jesus, to give hope in the midst of the squall. People need to know they can't control the storm, but they can surrender their hearts and lives to the One who can.

I don't think it's possible to be downtrodden and miserable all of the time—to consider yourself a victim and thrive on neglect— if you know Jesus. It's an oxymoron.

So many people are hurting, but too many people believe they have no purpose but to suffer. Too many people only know how to live as victims. These folks need hope and restoration, but many of us are so worried about offending someone with our faith that we don't tell them about the sweet, marvelous righteousness available through Jesus.

Tell someone what Christ has done for you—how He pulled you out of the pit, how He healed your body, how He restored your joy, how He answered your prayer, how He covered you with peace, how He delivered you from evil, how He created a clean heart within you, or how He made you righteous.

It's your job to shout victory from the rooftops.

THINGS THAT WORK
MY NERVES #4

Holiday shopping

Going to the crowded grocery store on Christmas Eve,
I always pray I leave with French's Crispy
Fried Onions instead of a felony.

Chapter Twenty-Three

God's Oath

I've been pregnant the entire time I've worked on this book. The laptop has shaken and shimmied from the precious baby kicking and hiccupping in my stomach. But now she's here. She's two weeks old today as she lies on my chest, breathing softly and cooing. I close my eyes and take in the sweet scent of her pink skin and dark hair. She's our miracle baby—our surprise. She's our sweet Annabeth.

In *Can't Make This Stuff Up!* I wrote in detail about my infertility struggles. It wasn't until three months after I completed the manuscript that I found out I was pregnant. I had just returned from being a chaperone at my daughter's church camp and was as nauseated as I could be. I assumed it was from three days of eating Tater Tots, but no. I don't have to tell you that I nearly fainted when I saw the second line appear on the pregnancy test.

For six years I'd petitioned God about my deep yearning for another child. I was blessed with a fertility doctor who prayed along with me at appointments. I prayed every time I saw an ultrasound photo and read a pregnancy announcement on social media, every time I threw a negative test in the trash, every time I passed the baby department in Target. I'd prayed for her by name: Annabeth, meaning "favor, God's oath." I waited. I wrote my desire in my prayer journal and drew circles around it. I hit my knees. I knelt at the altar. I lifted my hands. I prayed. Friends prayed. Strangers prayed.

And now here she is. On my chest. Breathing softly. Every tear and every prayer answered.

Here she is.

A lifetime is but a whisper to the Lord, and my six years of begging was just a flash to Him. In His infinite wisdom and perfect timing, He waited to give me this precious girl. It's a little ironic because my mother was thirty-six when I was born, and I always poked fun at her for being older than my friends' moms. I made jokes about tennis balls on the legs of her walker and feeding her baby food. And now that I'm thirty-seven years old, the Lord has given me the baby I longed far. I'm waiting for my payback. I'm waiting for tennis balls in wrapping paper at Christmas.

I've been discouraged so many times over the last six years. I've had well-meaning friends tell me I should move on—that God was telling me no. I've been plagued with uncertainty. In an earlier chapter I mentioned the doubt the devil placed in my mind when I wrote scriptures with promises of Sarah's conception on the studs of our home and when I designated a room for a nursery.

Yet somehow I held on to the vision. I held on to what I believed God had promised me—the vision of a blue-eyed baby in my arms. The desire was just so strong, God-ordained, that when doubt crept in, I rebuked it with truth.

And here she is. Conceived without medication. Placed in my womb at the perfect time. I declare the Lord has great plans for her.

Annabeth smiles all the time. She's only two weeks old, but she does. I don't want to believe it's gas. After all, I never smile when I have gas—or when Jason has gas either. I want to believe she's dreaming of her time in heaven before she was born, when she was with my parents and grandparents, the soul I miscarried at six weeks, and even my sweet Newt. She's dreaming of Jesus whispering blessings into her ear. Or because somehow she knows she's the fulfillment of a promise—as I believe she is.

When the Maker of heaven and earth makes an oath to you, nothing has the power to break it. He promised Elizabeth and Sarah they would have children when Sarah's eggs were older and more scrambled than mine. He promised to deliver His people from Pharaoh. He promised victory at Jericho. There are over seven thousand promises in the Bible, and not one went unfulfilled. (I didn't count the promises personally, but I did enough reading and research (that is, googling) to feel confident it's true.

Let's not confuse God's promises with worldly success or simple wish fulfillment. Just because we want something doesn't mean it is an oath from God. "God promised I'm going to make a quick million before I'm forty. He said I will buy a private island and hire Matthew McConaughey to play the bongos while I sunbathe."

The Lord does bestow prosperity on His believers, but on His terms, for His own purposes. He definitely doesn't guarantee that all Christians will dance around on a yacht in monokinis with diamonds in a champagne glass like a rap video. More often, He simply provides.

My mother made very little money during the last years of her life, but God always took care of her. Sometimes she'd get a random refund check she didn't expect, or the store would take back her antique hair dryer (kidding). And somehow she was able to purchase a lovely home, always have a car to drive, and have all of her needs met. Mama never had a mansion or yacht on this earth, but God fulfilled His promise to care for the widow (Deut. 10:18; Ps. 68:5; Isa. 54:5).

God sometimes tells us no. He sometimes tells us not yet. But when He promises something will come to fruition, it will. It may take forty years, as it did for those Hebrews aimlessly wandering around the desert. It may take six years of praying for a child. Sometimes it may be fulfilled in ways we haven't anticipated. But when God has truly made an oath, He will fulfill it. He won't go back on it. He's not a deadbeat dad who leaves his kids waiting on the porch steps with a packed suitcase and a beach towel to go to the water park and never shows up. He's a good, good Father.

How do we know if God has promised us something? If it's in Scripture, we can trust it. But God's promises can also come through a constant nudge, a little voice. That's the way it was for me with Annabeth. When I was ready to give up on the idea of a third child, I would just feel something—something indescribable—saying to me, "I will grant the desire of your heart."

> ✦ **When God has truly made an oath, He will fulfill it. He won't go back on it.** ✦

And I said yes! Even when I wasn't sure it was true or couldn't tell if it was just my own mind saying those things, I claimed it aloud. I spoke life. I spoke the promise aloud. I claimed scriptures. I also prayed that if what I was sensing *wasn't* a true promise from God, He would take away the longing to have another child. But He never took it away. As I aged and my eggs shriveled up and died and new crow's feet and dark spots covered my face, the yearning only grew stronger. And then, eventually, there was Annabeth.

In my life I've had several dreams, several nudges, like this.

When I was in elementary school, I used to stand in the living room and preach to my mama and my stuffed animals sitting on the couch. I told them they needed to be the hands and feet of Jesus. I told them a mission field waited right outside the front door and they needed to do something for the kingdom, glory to God! I'd get all fired up, a chubby ten-year-old white girl, and shout and holler like T. D. Jakes. My stuffed pink puppy dog, Rascal, would get all fired up, too, and wave his handkerchief in the air and let out a hearty "Amen!"

Mama told me after those "sermons" that she believed I was called to preach. I didn't think much of it. I was just playing pretend. I was going to be a writer when I grew up, not a preacher. God had already given me the desire to write at a very young age, and that's what I was going to do. I had that vision, too—of signing books as an adult.

But twenty-seven years later, God has allowed me to merge those very things. The first time I was asked to stand behind a pulpit and preach to a women's ministry, I couldn't help but think of those times I'd played pretend in the living room. My mother had already passed away, but I imagined her and Rascal sitting in the front pew. God was preparing me, so very long ago, for what He wanted me to do as an adult. He gave me a vision at the age of eight and brought it to fruition at the age of thirty-six.

Another vision I often had over the years was of a house. It was white brick with black shutters, surrounded by beautiful aged oaks. Rocking chairs and ferns lined the porch, and blond children played in the grass. These days, when I pull up our long driveway and see that vision come to life, I can do nothing but thank Him.

There were other visions, too—visions of being the bride of a particular boy I worshipped in high school, for example. That didn't come to fruition, praise God, and that's one of those things Garth Brooks sings about in "Unanswered Prayers." Not all of our visions come to pass, and that's His perfect will too.

Still, God gives the perfect desires of our hearts to those who love Him—to those who humble themselves before Him and say, "I can do nothing, have nothing, achieve nothing—without You, God. Every good gift comes from Your hand." My visions of this home and this child and even this book sitting on a shelf at Barnes & Noble were part of my dreams and prayers for decades.

I have other dreams and prayers that have not yet been answered. I'm still drawing circles around some bold petitions to God. That may be true for you too. Your visions, your desires, may not have come to pass.

But sister, we serve a faithful Father who hears our pleas. He knows our hearts. He knows our longing. He will always give the perfect answer—either yes, no, or not yet.

He's a God who makes dreams become a reality. He's a God who exceeds expectations. He's a God who provides and restores. He's a good God who does abundantly more than we could ever ask or think. For that I'm so incredibly thankful.

If you have what you believe to be a God-ordained promise and vision in your life, cling to it. Don't let the naysayers say nay. Don't let Satan steal your hope. If your dreams and your deep desires threaten the devil, he's going to do all he can to kill them. Do you think the devil wants to see you succeed or do work for the kingdom or be fulfilled? Heck no. Satan loves broken dreams and disappointment.

If you're confident God has promised you something—if scriptures continually point you to that promise and it's a constant nudge on your heart, then don't lose hope. Rome wasn't built in a day, they say. Jericho's walls didn't fall in a day. The Hebrews didn't get out of the desert in a day. This sweet baby on my chest was hundreds of days and prayers in the making. The wait is worth it with God.

THINGS THAT WORK
MY NERVES #1

My sin

Chapter Twenty-Four

WWJD

While writing this book, I often prayed that it not be contradictory. I never want to be accused of leading anyone astray or using Scripture to suit my own wants and needs. (Side note: I've worn a spot on the backspace button of my keyboard. Thank You, God, for wisdom, discernment, and conviction.) The Bible clearly tells us to love others, and yet I don't. The Bible also tells us to be content in all situations, and I'm not. As you've read thus far, you'll know that I'm not joyful or even pleasant and loving to be around when Walmart has more lanes full of people than the interstate or when I am forced to interact with people I deem difficult. And, as a follower of Christ, I am supposed to freely give grace and mercy, aren't I? After all, I'm certain God has shaken His head a couple of times at my thirty-seven years of shenanigans. And yet He sent His Son to die for me anyway.

Years ago, I worked with a girl who drove me stark-raving mad. I'm not a morning person, and she was. Her cheerful disposition at the butt crack of dawn made me want to throw my coffee mug against the wall and then grind the broken bits of glass into her eyeballs. I once told my mother, "Jesus may love her, but she drives me nuts."

Now, is that anything a follower of Christ should say? Absolutely not. In fact, I should have strived to be more like her instead of angrily slamming my purse down at my desk every morning with sleep boogers in my eyes and a ticked-off look on my face.

My Grandmaw Lucy was a sweetheart. Everyone who knew her described her as a "fine Christian woman." However, she once told my mother, "Susan, I just don't like people." By the time she was seventy-five, she was tired of people. She was tired of their idiocy. She was tired of foolishness. She was tired of this world and its sin. She was tired of watching the news every evening, only to be grieved at the stories she saw. She was ready to go to heaven, and soon after she said those words to my mama in a Taco Bell drive-through, she did.

Were my grandmother's thoughts and words about others that day pleasing to God? I don't know.

Do you remember the WWJD bracelets that were so popular in the nineties? Each time I looked down at the question on my wrist, I felt incredible pangs of guilt for continually rolling my eyes at situations or cussing out someone who made me mad. Instead of repenting and changing my behavior, though, I just quit wearing the bracelet. I took the easy route (and often still do).

But it's a wonderful question, isn't it? What *would* Jesus do?

What would He do if He passed a woman in the store wearing Tweety Bird pajama pants? Well, He'd know her life's story. He'd know the state of her soul. He also might know that her father had called her in the middle of the night because her mother was being rushed to the hospital by ambulance. Jesus would know she was in such a frantic state that she didn't change out of her pajamas before running to her mama's side. Jesus would know she'd just left the hospital and was in the store buying toiletries for her father to have as he sat beside his dying wife and held her frail hand. Jesus would know the specifics, and He wouldn't dare shake His head at her ensemble.

Ouch.

There's one strike against me—and maybe against you if you said amen to my rant about pajama pants in public.

What would Jesus do if He was stuck in traffic construction? Would He mouth off and blow the horn and make an obscene gesture out of His sunroof to the road crew fixing potholes in the fast lane? He wouldn't. He would pray blessings over the DOT workers. He would smile and know this delay in traffic would ultimately prevent a horrific accident when the eighteen-wheeler two miles ahead blew a tire. This delay was literally a lifesaver.

Your Facebook rant about the traffic jam seems rather foolish now, doesn't it?

I don't think the Lord minds our humor or even our rants, but I know He minds hatred. He's a God of love, and in 1 John 4:20 we read that if we say we love God but we hate our brother, then we are liars.

God knows my heart, and He knows that my jokes and criticisms don't come from a place of hatred. I don't say that to justify myself or imply that I can do and say whatever I want as long as I think it's okay. I know people are watching me. They are holding me accountable. They are really quick to call me one of those "judgmental Christians" if I take it too far.

But making jokes has always been my forte. In school, friends would say to me, "Susannah, make me laugh." I could usually come up with something on the spot, and sometimes it would be at the expense of the cafeteria lady's ill-fitting hairnet or an impression of our American history teacher's raspy voice. I only meant to provide a little irreverent humor to lighten a burden or bring a smile to someone's face.

Was my way of cheering up others pleasing to God? Again, I don't know.

I do know this.

In Luke 6:27–36 we are told to love the unlovable. What good is it to only love those people who love us? To only love those we can tolerate? To only love those who never disagree with us? To only love those who vote the way we vote or think the way we think? To only love those who never wear white after Labor Day? That's easy stuff. Loving those who work our nerves is hard, but that's where the reward is found. I'm sure I've missed out on plenty of blessings by not adhering to that scripture.

It *is* hard. It's hard following Christ. It's hard to be His representative on earth. It is easier to say and do whatever our flesh tells us to say and do. It's easier hating our enemies and viewing ourselves as superior to anyone who doesn't dress the way we do or believe what we believe. It's easier to get angry and impatient than to view trying situations the way Christ would view them. It's easier to crack cruel jokes than to think of the feelings of others.

By the same token, it's easier to be offended than to overlook what others say and do. It's also easy to keep our mouths shut for fear of offending someone, which causes us to fail at being His bold representatives.

I struggle with it. I struggle with extending grace toward those who work my nerves. All I know to do is to pray fervently for God to convict me if I take things too far or if my humor becomes hatred.

Years after this book is published and resting on bookshelves across America, I may pick it up one rainy day, and God may speak to my heart, "Whoa! Susannah. You shouldn't have written that, dear. What in the world were you thinking?" And all I'll be able to say is, "Lord, I'm sorry."

Being a Christian is hard, yet it's such an important calling. It's a great responsibility, and it's rewarding in ways we will see both on this earth and long after we're in heaven. It's fulfilling when we learn from our mistakes. It's a testimony when we're able to tell others about all the times we've come up short in the past, but God changed our mind and our heart.

Don't misunderstand. Not all humor is bad—not even all irreverent humor. I think I've made Jesus chuckle a time or two. I think the laughter in my household and my ability to parody songs makes Him smile. I think one of His gifts to me was my sense of humor. When someone tells me that I've made them laugh on a bad day, I delight in that. More important, I think He delights in that too.

I'm actually a lot like Grandmaw Lucy. I don't like a lot of people. (Except for *you*. I love *you*.) I don't like the ways of this world and its sin. I don't like being treated rudely by cashiers or being overcharged for bananas at the grocery store. I don't like receiving derogatory comments on blog posts that tear apart my beliefs. I don't like invasion of my privacy. I don't like running into ex-boyfriends when my hair is greasy and I have a zit on my chin. I don't like the attitude of entitlement that some kids possess today. I don't like coyotes. I don't like the overly offended. I don't like seeing children glued to screens instead of climbing trees. I don't like doubt and fear and all the garbage Satan dumps in our minds. I don't like garages crowded with junk. I don't like grocery store remodels. I don't like the trials and tribulations of this fallen world. I don't like commercials that tell us the phone number to call nineteen times in a row.

There's just some stuff I don't like.

But I do love Jesus.

And He's the only one I'm worried about offending.

> There's just some stuff I don't like. But I do love Jesus. And He's the only one I'm worried about offending.

Acknowledgments

Thank you, Lord, for giving me the desire to write and the opportunity to share it with others.

Thanks to the entire Thomas Nelson team—including but not limited to Jenny, Stephanie, Lauren, Shea, and Janene—for every ounce of energy you put into me and this book. You are so talented in what you do, and I would be clueless without each one of you.

Thanks to my agent, Jessica Kirkland, for the hours of communication and advice and laughs via voice messages, texts, and phone calls. There's no doubt the Good Lord placed you in my path. You are such a pivotal part in my childhood dream becoming a reality.

Thanks to my family for allowing me to share our lives with strangers. I hope this doesn't contribute to any future therapy sessions.

Thanks to every follower and fan on social media who has supported and encouraged me along the way.

For anyone I forgot to acknowledge, I hope you aren't offended.

About the Author

Susannah B. Lewis is a humorist, blogger for Whoa! Susannah, and freelance writer whose work has appeared in numerous publications. The author of *Can't Make This Stuff Up!*, Lewis lives in Tennessee with her husband, Jason, their three children, and six (yes, six) dogs.